James Likins

Six years experience as a book agent in California

Including my trip from New York to San Francisco via Nicaragua

James Likins

Six years experience as a book agent in California
Including my trip from New York to San Francisco via Nicaragua

ISBN/EAN: 9783337147976

Printed in Europe, USA, Canada, Australia, Japan

Cover: Foto ©Andreas Hilbeck / pixelio.de

More available books at **www.hansebooks.com**

BOOK AGENT

IN CALIFORNIA,

INCLUDING

My Trip from New York to San Francisco via Nicaragua.

By MRS. J. W. LIKINS.

SAN FRANCISCO.
Women's Union Book and Job Printing Office, 424 Montgomery Street.
1874.

Entered according to Act of Congress, in the year eighteen hundred and seventy-four.
By MRS. J. W. LIKINS,
In the Office of the Librarian of Congress, at Washington.

PREFACE.

Unlike most authors, who dedicate their books to some dead or absent friend, or dear relative, I will dedicate this work to my creditors, hoping that my friends and readers may be amused and benefited sufficiently to compensate them for their time and trouble in its perusal; while at the same time I hope to be benefited by the sale of the work sufficiently to satisfy all demands of my creditors, and have a few almighty dollars left, for my time and labor, as well as expense, in bringing it before the public.

It is not my intention to discuss the merits of this work in the few prefatory remarks I shall make, but will leave it to a generous public to decide; and sincerely hope those who have patronized me as a book agent, will not fail me now, since I have turned authoress.

THE AUTHOR.

SAN FRANCISCO, 1874.

SIX YEARS EXPERIENCE
AS A BOOK AGENT
IN CALIFORNIA.

CHAPTER I.
From New York to Greytown.

Akron, Summit Co., Ohio, March 26th, 1868.
No. 225 South Summit street.

All is bustle and confusion. We are making preparations to move; for we have sold our house, and must give possession by the first of April.

When I look around the grounds, although every thing is covered with a slight fall of snow, I think how many happy hours I have spent in planting flowers and training vines.

Now I must leave them all, with their pleasant memories. There, too, is the grape arbor, where my husband, children and I have spent so many pleasant moments. Also, the four large maples, outside the gate. They are very dear to me; for the one that planted them sleeps in an unknown grave on the battlefield of the Wilderness.

The neat iron gate, where Jack, the watch-dog, during the hot summer afternoons would wait for the return of my little girl from school, to take him down to the canal for a bath, which was three blocks away.

He now stands looking up in my face, as though he, too, *knew* we must part.

But I must cheer up; for I see my husband coming, pale, and nearly tired out; with him is my dear friend and neighbor, Mrs. F. She said, "I have almost persuaded Mr. L. to go to California with us; that is, if I can get your consent. The sea voyage will do you all good; and the climate is so fine you would like it, and have better health, I am sure. What do you say, Mrs. L.?" I replied, "If it is as you say, I would not mind going. Any place, but to Tennessee. I am not afraid on my account, but you know Mr. L. is such a strong republican, and the feeling against them hasn't died out yet in the South; they might mob him. Anyhow, he wouldn't do well in business there. *Of course*, I would just as lief go to California, for we are broken up here; at least, there won't be much left when our debts are paid."

At this she seemed very much surprised, and said, "Why, I thought you were worth thousands." "No, indeed," I replied, "not now. I would not have sold my home if there was any help for it, but I wish to pay my just and honest debts and go among strangers; for we will have to make a new beginning."

Turning to Mr. L., I said, "Will you go?"

He replied, "I would like to, but can we get ready?"

"Yes, of course we can; it is five days until Mrs. F. and her husband leave here for New York. We will unpack our furniture, sell what we can at private sale, and the rest at auction."

"All right—we will go."

Mrs. F. left, very much delighted, to tell her husband.

For the next five days I had no time scarcely to think.

Neighbors calling and offering their assistance; buying some little nicknacks they knew I prized, saying they would keep them for remembrance.

By the 31st, all our household furniture was disposed of in some way. We spent the night with a friend of ours. The next day my friend, with the assistance of Maria, a girl I had in my employ, prepared lunch enough to last us until we arrived in New York. I must here say, I hated to part with Maria, as she had been in my employ for over a year, and had proved herself kind and faithful to me in sickness and health. I would have liked very much to have taken her with me, as she was a poor, homeless creature.

The hack called in the afternoon to convey us to the depot. After our trunks are strapped on, the satchels stowed away, and last, but not least, the lunch basket, we bid good bye to poor old Jack, whom my little girl had given to our friend's son, who had promised to take good care of him.

Arriving at the depot, we found many friends awaiting to see us off. Among them was an old gentleman, who had been in California in '49. In describing the place to me, how rough and uncivilized the people were *there*, he almost discouraged me.

Mr. F. and wife got to the depot just as the train came up.

With many tears we bid our friends good bye, for years and perhaps forever. Who knows?

We had not traveled very far, when F. very jovially said, " Mrs. L. and my wife's noses are as red as though they had been on a spree for a month," at which we laughed through our tears.

We pass many towns and villages; at one of the

stations a young gentleman who used to board with me came into the car to bid us good bye.

I now had time for reflection. I thought of the strange country we were going to, and of the strange faces we would see. My little girl, for a time, seemed to feel as badly as any of us; but, like all children, she soon forgot her trouble in the new scenes around her.

When the cars stopped for the passengers to take supper, we spread our cold lunch on the seat, which served as table, while Mr. F. took cups out, and soon came back with some nice hot coffee.

This style of eating was somewhat new to me. I must confess I rather liked it. But now my whole life must change. After the remains of the lunch were stowed away, and chatting for some time, we commence making arrangements for sleeping. I, for the first time, tried to make beds out of seats in a railroad car. Turning two seats facing each other, spreading blankets and folding shawls for pillows, I pack away my husband and child.

Rolling myself in a shawl, I soon fell asleep.

We were all awakened in the middle of the night by my husband laughing loudly. He lay with his heels on one seat, his head was on another, while he had a *seat* on the floor. He was so convulsed with laughter, that it was sometime before he could get strength enough to get up. After this, we slept very little.

Nothing of importance occurred until we reached S———, where we left the Atlantic and Great Western Rail Road for the New York and Erie. Now, for the first time, I began to realize what a trouble our bundles and satchels were. Here we all had quite a scare. In my hurry to get everything on the train, I dropped a shawl under the cars; as I was trying to get it the cars started, and had it not been for a gentleman pulling me out, I should have been crushed to death.

At last we are safely seated, and are off again. I could not help but laughing, whenever I thought how awkward I must have appeared when the gentleman pulled me out, for I had dropped my hat, and my water-proof cloak was partially off.

It was half-past four when the train stopped at Jersey City. Messrs. L. and F. left us in the ladies' sitting-room with the baggage, while they went across to New York to purchase the tickets and engage the staterooms, supposing we could go aboard the steamship that night, as it was advertised to sail next day.

At the steamship office they were told that the regular boat on the opposition line had proved, at the last minute, not seaworthy. In consequence, another one had to be repaired, and could not sail for several days.

They, however, purchased the tickets, but could not go on board to get staterooms until next morning, as the ship was anchored out in the East River.

Mrs. F. and I, waiting for them in Jersey City, thought they would never come; woman-like, we imagined that all sorts of things had befallen them.

We did not dare to leave the baggage to go and look for them, so we would each take all we could carry and stand outside waiting.

I guess, from the way people stared at us, they thought we *were trying* to emigrate to *some* place, but we did not know exactly *where* to.

The men came at last. To our inquiry as to what kept them so long, was, they had been trying to find cheap lodgings.

When we got to the place, I did not wonder at their staying so long, because it seemed to me as though we had been two hours coming over from Jersey City.

Everything about the house had the appearance of a third class hotel, even to the landlord and landlady.

The latter was a little dirty, dried-up old woman, looking more like a witch than anything I know of, while the former was a tall, raw-boned, rough fellow, and looked as though he had whiskey enough aboard to commit almost any crime.

The landlady showed us several rooms, out of which we chose one in the third story, with four beds in it, because we all wanted to be in one room, as we did not like the looks of the people that were around.

After putting our baggage into the room, we descended to the dining-room. The supper that was set before us was filthy in the extreme.

There was a plate of dried apples for dessert that looked as though the flies had roosted on them every night for a week, and brought to my mind some poetry I once knew:

> The farmer takes his gnarliest fruit,
> 'Tis wormy, bitter, and hard, to boot;
> They leave the hulls to make us cough,
> And don't half take the peelings off.
> Then on a dirty cord they're strung,
> And from some chamber-window hung;
> There they serve a roost for flies,
> Until they're ready to make the pies.

I arose from the table, having ate but a few mouthfuls; went to the room and devoured the remainder of the lunch we had not disposed of.

The first thing the gentlemen did next morning was to start out and procure new lodgings. They soon returned, saying they had found two nice rooms over a restaurant, where we could eat our meals. In a very short time we took possession of our rooms, and found them pleasant and comfortable. After partaking of a nice breakfast, we went out in a small tug-boat to the "Guiding Star," the steamer we were to sail in.

Although I had traveled a great deal on steamboats, this is the first time I was ever inside of a *steamship*. I thought *then* it was a beautiful ship, and very handsomely furnished; but since then, I have seen others far superior. On board everything was neat and clean. There were but few staterooms in the first cabin that were not taken. Not knowing anything about the motion of the ship *then*, we engaged one with a single and double berth in the stern end of the vessel.

After we had made all necessary arrangements, we went ashore and spent several days looking at the sights around the City. On the morning of the 6th of April, bright and early, we were on board the "Guiding Star," watching the passengers as they came aboard. In the afternoon the vessel went as far as the mouth of the river, where it remained all night, the fog being so thick the captain was afraid to venture out to sea until next morning.

On the 7th I was awakened by the motion of the ship, for she pitched terribly. Dressing myself and little girl, we went into the ladies' cabin to await my husband, as the stateroom was too small for three to dress in at the same time. In a few minutes he came out, looking very much refreshed by his night's rest. We all ascended to the deck.

I, for the first time, stood on deck of a steamship. The scene looked grand to me. In the distance, the land fading from view, while, in another direction, as far as the eye could see, was spread the broad Atlantic, with its waves rolling, sending up the spray until it glittered in the morning sun.

I have visited many watering places; on its shores, from some elevated point, watched the rising sun as it sent its rays o'er hill and ocean; even the pale moon, with its mellow light. I have bathed in its surf, and viewed it from the tall lighthouse; still it never seemed half so grand to me as now.

I cannot express my feelings with words or pen, for the scene was both beautiful and sad. I was startled from my reverie by hearing a *peculiar* noise. I saw a gentleman leaning over the railing, looking very much as though he was drunk, and trying to heave up Jonah, or something else. Just then, my little girl staggered up to me, saying, "Oh mamma, I am so sick." I hurried her down stairs to the stateroom as quick as possible, where she made free use of the tin-pans fastened on to the side of the berth. Afterward she seemed to feel much better. Bidding her lie still, I went in search of my husband. I found him at the foot of the stairs, trying to hold up one of the beams. When he saw me he said, "I wish they would hurry about breakfast; I think I should feel better if I had a cup of strong coffee."

The gong soon sounded, and we took our seats at the table. Although it was nine o'clock, there were but few at the table. I suppose *some* of them were in their berths, trying to play *drunk*. Mr. L. ordered coffee, but before the waiter returned, he started for the stateroom, walking like a blind horse, stepping very high, as though he thought the floor would come up and strike him in the face. I followed him to the stateroom, where he crawled into the upper berth, as my child was still in the lower one.

He also made good use of the tin-pan, spattering it all around. I felt sorry for them, but could not help smiling at the scene. Looking up, I saw Mr. F. standing in the open doorway, nearly bursting with laughter.

Upon inquiring for Mrs. F., he said she was in the same fix, and wanted to see me. I found her very sick, and tried to cheer her, by telling *her* what *she* told me, before we started, that sea sickness was good for a persons health, and would propably be beneficial to her; also told her, if there was anything I could do to assist, I would.

Thanking me, she said she only wanted to see if I was sick. For two days, my husband and child were very sick. On the third, they were a little better, but still could not sit up. Mr. L. being very weak, I was somewhat uneasy about him.

The stewardess told me they would *never* get any better until they went on deck. I started, determined to find some one to help me to get them there.

I found Mr. F. and wife, the latter having ventured on deck for the first time since she was taken sick. In answer to my inquiry as to her health, said she felt much better since she came out and walked around. I told Mr. F. I had come in search of some one to assist me in getting my folks out.

He said, "Where are his brother Odd-Fellows and Masons, why don't you call on them. You are always bragging about their kindness in sickness." "Yes, and I brag about them still. I shall find some of them, and ask for assistance." "All right," he said "I'll watch the proceedings."

I was now angry and hurt; I had not expected that from him. I turned to look for some one who wore an emblem.

For the first time since I had joined the Rebecca Lodge, fifteen years ago, did I need to make myself known.

At a distance, seated with some companions, was a man, I will not call him a gentleman, with three gold links fixed on his shirt-bosom. I spoke to him, and said, I would like his attention for a few moments. I tried to make myself known to him. He looked at me blankly for a second, then drawled out, "What is it you want old woman." This brought the tears to my eyes, at which one of the others said, "Why the old women is crazy."

As I was turning to leave them, a gentlemen touched me on the arm, and said, "Madam, can I assist you in any way?" I told him my situation. He frankly offered his assistance.

Mr. F. now came forward, and offered *his* services, telling me to stay with his wife, and asking my pardon for his abruptness. Taking several others with them, they went below, and soon returned with my husband and little girl; by using blankets and shawls, they were made very comfortable. Some kind gentleman ordered lunch for them on deck, of which then partook slightly; by night they were feeling much better.

In a few days my child was all right, and enjoyed running around the deck with other children.

My husband informed me the gentleman who had first offered his services was both a Mason and an Odd Fellow; he had noticed me trying to make myself known to that ruffian. We *now* had plenty of friends, who were ready to offer their assistance at all times.

Off Cape Hatteras we had quite a storm, making nearly everybody sick again. The measles broke out on board. How I pitied the poor women in the steerage, who had so many children, all sick at once; with very few comforts, and lots of filth and dirt. There was one old Jewish lady, who had nine children, that I took quite a fancy to. Although she was among such a rough crowd. I *know* she had seen better days. Several ladies and myself would often go with the doctor to see her, in his rounds in the steerage, and tried to add to her comforts in many ways. There was also a lady in the first cabin with five children; they were all sick about the same time.

The youngest being very delicate, did not live, but a few days after the body was dressed for its watery grave, the captain ordered it sewed in canvas.

It was placed on a plank, and held on the guards.

The passengers gathered round, the steamer stopped for a few seconds, while the chaplain repeated the burial services. The signal given the body was lowered to its last resting place.

The scene was sad and mournful. I did not wonder the mother looked almost heart-broken; but I suppose it *matters not* where we lay our loved ones, whether in the quiet family vault, the restless ocean or the bloody battle-field, or the neat lot in the cemetrey, where loved ones could plant flowers, and drop a tear on the marble slab, where their darlings lay. It matters not, for our souls shall meet again.

It is eleven days this morning since we left New York. There is quite a commotion on board, for the words are going around that we shall land in a few hours.

Every one is anxious to be the first to see land. Some mischievous chap, hollowed "Land, land!" and then laughed, after all had rushed to where he was standing.

But midst all this excitement the ship still plowed on for some time, before land was in sight. At first it seemed like a mere speck, but grew larger and larger as we approached it.

From the deck of the steamer, the country looked low and level. It seemed as though the sea was much higher. The ship cast anchor about four miles from Greytown; before she had hardly stopped, she was surrounded by natives with small boats, to convey the passengers ashore. The ladders were lowered. I stood anxiously watching the first boat load off. It was brought close as possible to the ladder, and the ladies would jump and be caught in the arms of the half naked natives, who would stow them away until he got his boat filled.

Four of them would take the oars and row away, while another would take the vacant place.

The third one at last pushed off, which contained Mr. F. and wife; they had insisted upon our accompanying them, but I could not get courage enough to venture just yet. As I watched their boat rise on some high wave, and then disappear for a moment, it seemed to me as though they would never reach land.

Several gentlemen had promised they would assist us in getting on, and go with us ashore. The fourth one had some trouble in getting passengers, as all were afraid to venture. The gentlemen said we might as well go now as any time; so we descended the ladder and were soon in the boat.

For some time the natives seemed to battle with the waves, but finally cleared the ship and rowed hard for the shore.

After being sprinkled several times by waves breaking over us, we reached the bar where they waited for a wave to carry us over.

In a few minutes we were raised high, and carried into the mouth of the river. I began to breathe more freely, although we were yet quite a distance from land. The boat moved more rapidly, an I we were now in very shallow water.
The natives had to push us ashore with setting poles.

When I once more found myself and family on land, I sent up thanks for our safety so far, to Him who rules over land and sea. I now began to look around me. At some distance I saw Mr. F. and wife coming toward us. When they came up, he said he had engaged lodgings for us in the same hotel with them.

Arriving there, we found the building a story and a half high, made of rough boards, with two long porches in front, the whole structure covered with a species of cane or palm, to make the rooms cool.

Everything outside had a free and easy appearance. Hogs running around the door, chickens on the porch, all seeming to be at home.

The landlord came forward, telling Mr. F. he could find the rooms. We passed up the rough outside stair, crossed the porch and entered a neat, though poorly furnished room, with a single and double bed. Although it was plain, I thought it was Paradise to being on the steamer; even then it seemed as though the house was pitching and rocking around.

We made good use of the soap and water, and dressed ourselves in suitable and comfortable clothing for this hot climate. Afterward we went below in search of the dining-room, in which we found a long rough table, minus a cloth, with long rough seats.

The fare consisted of roast pork, boiled rice, fried plantain and corn bread. They had some kind of wheat bread. I cannot call it any name, for I never saw anything like it before or since, but it answered for dessert with a cup of coffee.

The landlord was an old Californian, who was very polite and obliging, promising to show us around when it became cooler, saying we must not stir around much during the heat of the day for fear of fever.

Mr. F. and wife, myself and family, seated ourselves on the porch to watch the natives as they passed. The women wore dresses made of different kinds of thin material, hanging half off of them, showing all of their neck and shoulders, barefooted, while around their head they wore a very highly colored handkerchief, arranged in the same style as the negroes in the Southern States. They also looked free and easy.

The portion of the town we had a view of lay up the river. The houses were low and small, built of rough material, all covered with the same stuff as the hotel.

We all grew tired, and went to our rooms to rest ourselves, where I soon fell asleep. I was awakened by my little girl saying, "They are waiting for you mamma." I went below and joined the party. We started off, the landlord acting as guide. First we visited the foreign consuls. They received us very pleasantly. One of them had a beautiful cocoa-nut grove. Our guide showed us a great many native trees and shrubs, among them the orange, lemon, pine-apple, mango and plantain. I think the bread-tree the most beautiful of them all.

Its wide-spreading branches are of the handsomest green I ever saw, with its fruit in abundance. I did not taste it, as it was not ripe, but was told it tasted very much like our *wheat* bread.

We next visited the Marine burying-ground, which was some distance in the woods. On the way, we passed a low one story, odd looking building, with no windows. Our guide said it was where the Masonic lodge met. I wandered around the building; thought how different it was from the Temple I had visited not quite a year ago in Philadelphia. The one so very grand and this so lowly.

But I must follow the party.

On either side the paths, as they wind through the woods, are lined with wild flowers, and creeping ivy. At last we came to an opening in the woods, there, enclosed with a neat iron fence, lie the remains of many different nationalities, many of them had handsome tombstones placed there by their fellow seamen. We wandered around the woods for some time; they looked very dark and dismal, for it was now after sunset. It seemed to me as though a gloomier spot could not have been selected for a burying-ground.

We returned by the way of the river.

Our guide showed us the hull of an old vessel lying out on the bar, which he said belonged to Walker's fillibustering expedition.

We also saw the large warehouses where freight was stored. In this portion of the town the buildings are very good. There are two fine brick buildings owned by two Englishmen, who have large variety stores.

We returned to the hotel, and found, seated on the porch enjoying the evening air, many of the passengers.

The next morning before sunrise finds myself and family sitting on the river bank, with many others, watching how close the sharks would venture to land when anything was thrown in the water, frightening the children by catching them, and saying we would throw them to the sharks.

One thing seemed singular to me, how the half naked natives could swim or wade around in the water and the sharks would not trouble them, when they say it is hardly safe for white men to venture out in small boats. Several hours were quickly spent wandering around the shore, until time to return to the hotel for breakfast. when the landlord saw many of the ladies had on slippers. He told them they must not wear them out doors again, as they might get their feet full of jiggers.

He gave us a description of what they were. I remember seeing *some* of the toes of the natives partially eaten off. I asked him if they were the cause of that; he replied they were—that they sometimes made cripples of them.

After breakfast we lounged around the rooms and porches, until three o'clock in the afternoon; we then understood that the Moses Taylor was not expected until night. We knew we would not get away from Greytown for some days, as her passenger had all to be brought down the river before ours could go up. So in company with the landlord as guide, we started out sight seeing again.

Taking a different direction from the previous evening, we went around by the way of the Lagoon, where we stopped to look at the native women washing clothes. It was a novel way of washing to me. I therefore watched them with much curiosity; some were beating the clothes over logs, some superintending the boiling, while some were standing in the water rinsing, and others were spreading them on the grass and bushes to dry.

Leaving them to finish their work, we follow the lagoon for some distance farther on; the banks of which were very beautiful, covered with green grass.

with here and there a large tree, which made it cool and shady. We turned to the left and followed a path that led through a strip of woods towards the river. Close to the bank was a thicket of a species of cane ; here our guide told us to keep a sharp lookout, as the place was infested with many poisonous reptiles. For sometime we amused ourselves by getting water lilies and wild flowers, some of which were very beautiful, also quite fragrant.

We returned through the upper part of town.

Some of the natives had grounds enclosed around their dwellings, in which were planted coffee, indigo and other plants and shrubs, they seemed to be well cultivated and with some taste ; but the most of them had no enclosures about their dwellings ; around their doors were gathered monkeys, goats, chickens, pigs and generally half a dozen half naked, dirty children, all playing together, and looked as though they might eat and sleep in the same place.

Sickened with the sight, we returned to the hotel, where we found a young man, known among the passengers as 'Alabama', playing his pranks as usual and talking in his odd and droll way, telling negro stories such as this : "A very zealous colored sister being at a revival meeting, became very happy, and in her enthusiastic way, sprang upon her feet, and shouted very loudly, 'Oh Lord, I wish I had the wings of a june bug ; I'd fly to my Jesus.' Now a less enthusiastic brother, said, 'Hush, you fool ; the jay-bird would catch you before you got forty rods.'

He also told many more laughable ones. The next day was Sunday ; we did not go out much.

Monday morning they commenced to convey the baggage and steerage passengers down the coast, to the mouth of the Colorado river. The remaining passengers amused themselves by sitting on the bank, and watching them loading the small steamer until they moved away. We then dispersed to the different hotels, and made ready to go ourselves the next morning.

By ten o'clock the following day, the first and second cabin passengers were all aboard ; bidding good-bye to Greytown; we passed over the bar, and were once more on the ocean.

The steamer was a small coaster with no cabin or accomndations whatever. There was a heavy sea, and the little steamer seemed to have all she could carry, but still battled with the waves that seemed to threaten her destruction at any moment : at every surge she seemed to crack, and sound as though she would break to pieces.

She was named the 'Active', and I think it a very appropriate one too, for nearly all on board soon became very active, and seemed as though they would throw up even their boots; but I will not jest about it. All the benches were occupied by ladies, lying down, groaning and moaning.

The strongest man reeled, while others weaker soon became so sick that they lay on the bare floor, in all the filth and dirt—among them my husband. I was seated on some baggage, watching and tending my little girl, who was so white and limp I was afraid she would die. Two gentlemen came and took my husband on deck. I now began to feel sick, but my anxiety for my dear ones kept me up.

Soon those on deck were driven below. The word was given to fasten all the hatches while we crossed the bar, into the mouth of the Colorado river.

SCENE ON BOARD THE LITTLE "ACTIVE"

The pilot was lashed to the wheel, and even the brave, stout-hearted seamen looked pale, as they went around performing their duties. They said, "We were in great danger of being dashed to pieces. For a moment the steamer seemed to stop, everything was silent except now and then a groan from the sick. She seemed to rise on a wave, a grating sound, as though she struck bottom, then another rise, and she shot like a flash out into the mouth of the river.

The hatches were raised and all seemed to gain new life. We run alongside of the river steamer, and were soon on board, where we found the baggage and steerage passengers awaiting us. The two steamers now separated, midst many cheers for the safe return of the little 'Active' and its brave seamen.

CHAPTER II.

Crossing the Isthmus.

It was three o'clock; we were moving quite rapidly up the river. The boat was a long narrow structure, with a lower and upper deck, open at each side, with low guards. Through the centre were three rows of posts to which berths were attached, five or six feet apart, with canvass stretched wide enough for two persons, with one blanket and two pillows.

The passengers soon began to gather around an open window in the end of the boat, where lunch was given out. It consisted of cold boiled ham, bread and butter, canned monkey, or chicken, they said, and nice hot coffee.

The passengers had plenty of room in their stomachs, so they stored away a great quantity of it. I, for one, did not eat any of the fowl, as I did not like the looks of the bones; but some said it was delicious.

During the remainder of the afternoon we watched the shore eagerly to discover any birds or animals, but it was too late in the day, and none made their appearance.

The banks, on either side, were covered with heavy timber and under-brush, entwined with beautiful vines and flowers. In the setting sun it looked grand but gloomy.

Soon after dark the confusion began—stealing berths, and many other pranks. We had no light save the moon, and all laid down with our clothing on. I could distinctly hear Alabama's voice above the noise.

It seems he had stolen an old lady's berth, which she had left for a little while. He was saying to her, "Now, please, do go away, and let me sleep; you know I'm awful tired, that's a dear, good old soul." He then would make a hideous noise, like he was snoring. The lady became tired and disgusted talking, and undertook to pull him out, when he cried, "Help! Help! this old lady's trying to get in bed with me!" She now let him alone, when some kind gentleman offered her his berth. All was silent for some time and every one was thought to be asleep, when he yelled out, "Say, old lady, are you comfortable? 'kase if you ain't, I'll change with you."

Next morning when I awakened, the sun was shining brightly. Seats were at a premium. Those that had to stand would look over the side of the steamer very quietly, for sometime, then holler, "Alligator! Alligator!" Those occupying seats would, some of them, make a grand rush; but no alligator, nor anything else was to be seen; upon returning to their seats, would find some mischievous fellows in them, laughing heartily at the sport.

I could sit for hours watching the shore, admiring

the scenery. I was perfectly entranced with its beauty, but did not catch a glimpse of either beast or bird.

About noon we came to the foot of the rapids; here the steamer was made fast. It was said we were to remain until morning, while the steerage passengers walked around the rapids, and the baggage was conveyed in small boats. It was a wild and picturesque spot.

During the afternoon, in company with a small party, one acting as guide, who had been over the grounds before, we wandered through the woods for some time, but did not dare to venture far from the boat, for fear of wild beasts or savage natives. I saw many plants and shrubs in which I took great interest. Among them were the rubber and mahogany trees, the ginger root, and other plants. We returned without having seen a bird or monkey.

Several others, who had been out exploring, had exciting stories to tell: what wild animals they had seen, and how near they came being devoured.

Alabama, who, I think, had not left the boat at all, said, in his queer way, "Why, law, yes, I saw a flying angel wid de long, white robe."

Some of the passengers passed the time away fishing from the lower deck, with bent pins for fish-hooks. There were fish in abundance; a bread-crumb thrown into the water would create a perfect tumult. After they were fried by the cook, they tasted splendidly.

Next morning, at the first peep of day, we were on the move. The river was so low we had to go on foot around the rapids, while the sick and lame were taken in small boats. It was quite cloudy, and we had not gone far when a drizzling rain set in. We had prepared ourselves with umbrellas to protect us from the sun—now they became quite useful. The road, or path, rather, got very slippery and muddy, but Mr. F. and wife, myself and family got along nicely. We expected to rough it before we left Greytown. Some of the ladies had on long, trailing dresses and thin shoes, so they suffered the consequences.

But, for all the disagreeablenss, I enjoyed it. One-side of the narrow path was skirted with heavy woods, in which there were many birds, making the air resound with their merry notes. Once in awhile the chatter of some unseen monkey would be heard.

On the other side flowed the river. The path was so narrow we had to walk Indian fashion, one by one, which made quite a procession.

The distance was four miles from the steamboat we had just left, to the place where the next one was waiting for us. When we had walked two miles, we came to a low shed, where a native had ginger beer, whiskey and other drinks, also ginger-bread, green ginger-root and maple-sugar.

After resting for a while, and taking a glass of lemonade, we trudged on. It cleared off, and the sun came out warm—everything looked bright and cheerful. At length the remaining two miles were passed; we reached the head of the rapids. There was a short bend in the river; as we were now in sight of the steamboat, our party concluded to rest in this beautiful nook for a short time. The small boat containing the sick had not passed us yet, as they had to go very slowly, so there was plenty of time.

Seating ourselves on old logs and roots of trees, I thought a more beautiful place could not be found. It was so wild and everything grew with such luxuriance.

I do not think there can be any richer soil in the world.

The little boat was seen, after the lapse of a couple of hours, coming slowly up the river. Some of the natives were trying to row, while others were out in the water pushing with poles.

They soon passed us and ran alongside of the steamboat; the sick, lame and balance of the baggage were conveyed on board; we walked slowly up the river bank, until we came opposite the boat, where we passed down the gang-plank, and were soon on board.

As the little nook faded from our view it looked more beautiful than ever. While our boat steamed gallantly up the river, I watched both shores in hopes of getting sight of an alligator, and often imagined I saw one, but as the boat would approach near enough to get a good look, it would prove to be an old log, or piece of drift wood, lodged against the bank.

But after a good deal of watching and any amount of patience, almost exhausted, a regular, genuine live alligator, was discovered lying on a low gravelly bank, out some distance from the water, enjoying himself in a sound sleep in the bright sun. When the boat came near enough to wake him up, he leisurely betook himself to the water in a kind of half walk and half crawl manner, he seemed to be very awkward on dry land, however spry he may be in the water.

As a thing of beauty he is not a success, in my estimation, and looked but little different from the imaginary ones I had seen previous to this in the shape of old logs, &c.

The river along here was shallow and narrow, on account of the very low stage of water, and so very crooked and meandering in its course, that, as small as our boat was, it was almost impossible for it to follow the channel; in some places, often the pilot would run the bow of the boat so close to the bank in these sharp turns, that the captain would have to keep a gang of native boatmen on the bow with setting poles to push her away; at times even this method would fail and she would strike the bank and stick there.

The only remedy left, would be for this gang of men to plunge into the water, which was generally about waist deep, and with a tow line, pull her bow around from the bank by main force. These difficulties, of course, made our progress very slow, but slow as it was, it did not become irksome, for the climate was delightful, and the scenery was wild and beautiful enough to suit the most romantic maid of sixteen, or the greatest lover of nature in all her natural beauties.

The land on each side was covered with almost every variety of timber known to that country.

Underneath the trees were a great variety of plants, shrubs, and vines, some of which had climbed almost to the tops of the tallest trees, and were in full bloom, giving the forest on either side a most delightful appearance, but looked to me almost impenetrable to man or beast.

As I looked at this beautiful and rich country, lying idle and in a wilderness, I thought if it was under the protecting arm of the United States, how soon Yankee industry and skill would make it the garden spot of the New World; but so long as it remains under the control of the indolent natives, it will be just as it is, a half-civilized wilderness.

This boat was one grade smaller than the former

one, with fare and lodging; about the same sleeping on bare canvas, without any bed-clothes; but as the nights were very warm and pleasant, we did not feel like complaining; the food was passed out of the store-room through a small window. Your cup of coffee, and a tin plate of cold boiled ham and canned meat, with a piece of bread, must be received in your hands, and eat the best way you could, standing or walking around he deck, as there were no tables.

We only passed one afternoon and one night on *this* boat; the next day, about ten o'clock, came in sight of a small town, called Castillio; here we had to land again, at the foot of the rapids, and walk around, this time about one mile.

In going around the rapids, we passed through this little, dirty, filthy town, of a few low huts, covered with cane, all on one street, almost every house a trading shop of some kind; most of them, however, were drinking shops.

Just above the town, at the head of the rapids, was a fort, manned by a few native soldiers. I had a good opportunity to see a part of them, as a few of the passengers, getting some lightning whiskey at the numerous shops in town, became noisy, and it was said, abused some of the native dignitaries; whereupon they sent to the commandant of the fort for a squad of soldiers to quell the disturbance. He sent down about a dozen men, under the command of a commissioned officer, who marched them down through the one street of the town, with more pomp and display than ever Napoleon did his victorious army after a successful engagement. Some had old rusty muskets, and some only swords in about the same condition; they were all bare-footed, most of them bare-headed, with but a substitute for a military uniform.

The officer threatened to arrest nearly the whole boat load of passengers, but after a while, marched his brave troops back to their quarters, without making a single arrest.

We were then allowed to embark on board of another steamboat, lying above the rapids, waiting for us. We were soon on board, and got away from this great military city, without further adventure. We were told this was the place where General Walker's fillibustering expedition finally came to grief; which, I presume, was correct, as the hull of an old ship lay down the river, below the town, said to have been sunk by the fortifications at this place, and drifted down, and lodged, had formed quite a little island by earth and driftwood lodging against it.

This third boat was still smaller than the last, and the accommodations still poorer, or rather none a all, as there were not even canvass bunks, or no provisions on board; the boat looked to me as though it was rotten enough to fall to pieces by the motion of the engine; which would move back and forth every stroke as though it lay loose on the deck; however, we were not destined to remain long on this frail craft.

About nine o'clock we came in sight of the light on board of the lake steamer, and were soon along side ready to be transferred. It was very dark and foggy; the lanterns flickered so it was almost impossible to see. We were hurried on deck like so many cattle, and driven into a narrow hall in which there was no light except the lantern which our guide carried; the flickering light made the place look very dismal and uninviting. That night I never shall forget—even now as I pen these lines I shudder at the thought, how we grouped our way up the side of the steamer, along the dark passage way, while, in some distant portion of the steamer, could be heard the wild screams of a maniac.

As we were driven farther along, the screams grew louder and louder, until I imagined I could feel her long bony fingers clutching me. In the stem of the steamer I saw a pale stream of light shining through the blinds of her state-room. I was pushed by the crowd against the door, which made her scream louder than ever, while I stood trembling with fear, thinking she might spring out upon me. Some ladies were protesting against being driven any farther, when the Captain who was standing in the bow of the boat holding the lantern over his head, giving orders, said they need not be afraid as the lady was closely guarded and could not hurt any one.

It seemed a lifetime to me until the word was given that we could go to our state-rooms. Provision was made for the sick, first the ladies and children, next I, my little girl, and my friend Mrs. F. took possession of one. We found it very small, with two bunks, the lower one almost on the floor.

With a blanket, shawls and satchels for pillows, we soon retired for the balance of the night.

It was sometime, however, before I could get to sleep, for I could still hear the screams of that poor maniac, and while I lay there thinking what could have caused her insanity I fell asleep.

It was quite late the next morning when I awoke, it did not take long to complete our toilet, for our room was minus water, soap or mirror. I combed my hair as best I could and left the room.

When I stepped outside, I noticed the hall between

the state-rooms was long and quite narrow, without an article of furniture or a piece of carpet, and was very filthy and dirty.

I passed to the left, through a narrow door, which lead to the bow of the boat, when I found myself on what seemed to be a kind of promenade deck, something after the style of the river steamboats in the East, except this one was covered overhead.

Through the centre was a long, rough, narrow table, on one side of which was a bench of the same make and material; on it were seated a number of rough-looking native passengers, gambling, all more or less intoxicated.

As I leaned over the guards, looking into the water, I could hear the voice of the captain giving orders to the sailors—swear an oath for almost every word he said. I thought the whole place fearfully low and wicked; but our passengers soon began to gather around on the bow of the steamer.

I overheard a native, who could speak good English, tell one of our passengers, they were taking the insane lady from Castillo to Virgin Bay; that she had been forced to marry contrary to her wishes, and became insane.

We now came quite close to a large mountain, rising out of the lake, very rough and rugged in its appearance, with a cone-shaped top, in which seemed to be a cavity. Around the edges were dark craggy-looking points. We were told it was an extinct volcano.

While all were looking closely at it, I heard some one scream; upon turning around, saw a young lady, who went by the name of Miss S., had fainted and fallen into the arms of a nice-looking gentleman. He said he was single. Whether he was or not, it is as Lord Dundreary says, "That's something no fellow can find out." She did not frighten me much, for I had seen the performance too often while we were on board of the Guiding Star. But I could not blame her very much, as she was getting along pretty well in years, and, I should judge, from her actions, she would like to find some man who would marry her. She came to finally, and the excitement subsided.

The mountain was passed, and we concluded to have some breakfast; of this every one could partake freely, providing he *found his own grub*. Ours consisted of hard sea biscuits, native fruit, and river water, with lime juice in it for drink.

I bit very carefully on the hard biscuits, for fear I might break my false teeth. I did not wish to have another commotion on board, for if they were broken, there would be a wedding, for my nose and chin would meet.

The steamer now began to round in toward the shore. It was ten o'clock; she was some time in making the landing, for the passengers would rush to the bow of the boat, which would make her stick fast, before she could reach the rough pier, and would have to back out and take a new start. But after many trials, and a great deal of swearing, the captain succeeded in making a landing, and we were soon marched off on to the pier. We started for the town, which was a few hundred yards away, and when we arrived at Virgin Bay we stopped to take dinner. Here, and there, scattered through the town, were sheds made of brush, under which were rough tables. You could have your choice of them, but, to me, they all looked alike. I was too hungry to look around much, so my family and I were soon seated, devouring chicken, rice, boiled eggs, and hot coffee. I would have to stop, once in a while, to pick the largest pieces of dirt out of the bread, as I did not wish to choke. I told Mr. F. I did not want to be denied the pleasure of going out to the Moses Taylor in the little boats he had talked about. He had pictured them to me as more dangerous than anything we had yet encountered.

After dinner, we looked around the town for a little while, and met many natives with parrots and monkeys for sale. My husband bought one of the former for our little daughter.

The conveyance from Virgin Bay to San Juan del Sur consisted of old ambulance wagons, drawn by horses and mules. You could have your choice, to go on horseback, but the horse turned out to be a mule, or in a wagon. Many gentlemen chose the former.

Our party engaged an ambulance and paid the driver extra, for not to crowd it in. We had not gone more than three miles, when we would come upon some broken-down team, or see some mule trying very hard to get rid of its rider. Still farther on we saw some mules who had succeeded, making for home, to be hired out again, and the poor, unfortunate fellows would have to walk it out, unless they were taken in by some teams.

The road that lead down the mountain was very good; the scenery fine; so fine, indeed, I was sorry when we reached the foot and began to move slowly up the beach, where the few houses and sheds seemed alive with our passengers.

At a short distance from shore lay the Moses Taylor, like a mountain rising from the Ocean.

After alighting from the ambulance we went into

the sheds. There were many native women, with very handsome shells, bead-work and corals for sale.

Mr. F. said I had better hide Polly, as they do not allow them on board, which I did, by emptying the contents of a basket into a shawl and making a bundle of them.

I put poor Polly into the basket and tied a shaw over it. She would let people know we had her, by once in a while giving a loud squeak, or bobbing her head against the shawl.

Preparations were soon made to take us on board; which was done by ropes made fast to the shore, and ship, also attached to a barge; we were drawn alongside of the steamer.

Just a little while before reaching it, the wind took my hat off, which in turn took my net with it, thus leaving my hair flying. We were too near the foot of the ladder for me to think of my appearance.

Nearly all had ascended; I stood in one end of the barge with the bundle on my arm, the basket containing the parrot in one hand, my hat in the other; and my hair streaming in the wind, fearing to step from the barge to the ladder, encumbered as I was; some kind gentleman assisted me. Once aboard I found Mr. F, and wife, my husband and little girl all laughing heartily at me saying, " You look as though you were crazy".

I was angry with them, and stepped into the ladies cabin just as I was. The stewardess came along, and said ," Madam, you had better go below; you do not belong in here." I told her I *knew where* I belonged and took a seat. She looked at me with her piercing gray eyes as if she too thought I was crazy. I felt myself as though I might be.

Mr. F. secured our state-rooms. When once in the room I made a change in my appearance. We went on deck and amused ourselves watching the rest of the passengers get aboard, until dark.

I found the Moses Taylor not so fine a steamship as the Guiding Star. The accomodations were very few; although the captain and crew seemed to do all that lay in their power to make us comfortable.

When I went into the state-room, I found Polly fast asleep upon the perch I had made for her, which consisted of a case-knife, with the blade stuck in a crack in the side of the steamer, close to the ceiling. On this she made her voyage from San Juan del Sur to San Francisco, except for a little while, three times a day, when she was lifted down to take her meals of coffee and cracker.

I soon retired for the night, and fell asleep. Very early next morning, found my husband, little girl and myself on deck, anxious to see the sun rise. Here we found many ladies and gentlemen already seated around the guards, enjoying the delightful morning air; among them Alabama. He looked pale; and upon my inquiry, told me he was quite sick, and would like very much to be with his mother this morning. I asked if there was anything *I* could do for him. "Not anything, I thank you," he said.

I crossed over to the opposite side, where Mrs. F. was sitting; after bidding her good morning, and enquiring after her health, I turned my gaze toward sunrise; for it now began to show its rays on the sky. The scene soon was very grand.

Far out on the peaceful Pacific was first seen a small, bright ray, which gradually grew brighter and brighter, until it became so brilliant you could not look upon it

GOING ON BOARD THE "MOSES TAYLOR"

with the naked eye, while close to the sides of the steamer the sprays would glitter in the sun.

I was startled from my reverie by some one pushing me so severe that I nearly lost my balance. On looking around, there stood Alabama, with his arms stretched out as though he was ready to catch me, and tried to look frightened; and drawled out, "Why, I guess you were asleep, or at least you were nodding, and came mighty near falling overboard. You frightened me terribly."

I told him I would thank him to keep his hands to himself. He said. "Well, I'll declare, that is the way you *thank* me, is it, for trying to save your life?"

The gong sounded, and we all went below to breakfast. Our seats had not been assigned to us yet, so we each took one, where we could find a vacancy. The fare was not as good as on the Guiding Star; still it did very well, and there was plenty of it.

During the day, my husband introduced me to the Captain, who by the way, is now chief wharfinger in San Francisco. He also introduced me to the first mate. I found them very pleasant gentlemen, but different in dispositions; the Captain firm, sedate, with but little to say, yet very kind and agreeable; while the other was jolly, full of fun, and always ready to play some prank.

In the evening nearly all were collected on deck; some amused themselves by dancing to the music played by an Italian, on a harp; others promenading, while I stood apart, watching the moon shedding her light over the smooth waters. The dancing ceased, and the Italian played a low, mournful air; I think it sounded more beautiful than anything I ever heard. It is true that music sounds the sweetest when on the rippling sea. It was very late before we retired that night, for it was so warm and pleasant on deck that many preferred it to the close, sultry state-rooms.

Several days passed without much change. The same monotonous life of a sea voyage. A great deal of the time when land was in sight, the Captain would explain points of note.

Longing for a change of some kind, I went with my husband, Mr. F. and wife below, to look around with the second mate for a guide; he took us down by the way of the cattle-pens and poultry coops.

The cattle were slaughtered every day to supply the tables of the steamer with fresh beef. They looked as though they had been fed on barrel hoops and moonshine. I thought it was a mercy to those that were killed first.

We then went through the engine room, and looked at the working of the powerful engine that propelled the steamer, and wondered at the immense amount of coal consumed by it while performing its work.

We returned on deck again, by the way of the steerage passengers' dining room. Their tables were composed of rough boards, hanging by iron rods, or hooks, attached to the ceiling; the passengers were just taking their dinner, and looked more filthy and dirty than the stock we had left.

The tables were furnished with tin plates, tin cups, iron spoons, knives and forks. The grub was served in a number of large tin pans, sitting along in the centre of the tables; it consisted of fat pork and beans, also bean soup. They drank a very poor quality of water, but seemed to relish their meal as well as if it was the best the ship could afford, served up on chinaware and a spotless table-cloth.

After our return on deck, my friend, Mrs F. and myself, went to the first mate's quarters to try and get a drink of good water; we found him pleasant and agreeable; he gave us a drink of condensed sea water, which we found quite an improvement on the supply of fresh water on board. He said he used it altogether for his own use, as he preferred it to any other he could get.

While talking, the surgeon passed; he gave us an introduction, and we learned that Alabama was quite sick; he took us to see him; we found his stateroom very close and uninviting. We took the doctor's orders concerning the medicine, and said we would act as nurse until he was able to be around again. Although he was such a wild harum-scarum fellow, I had taken quite an interest in his welfare. I learned that his parents were wealthy Southern people; he was well educated, but had run away from home for some reason or other.

Next day, Mrs. F. and I, in company with the doctor, paid a visit to our Jewish lady-friend in the steerage. We found this apartment smaller and dirtier than on the Guiding Star. She was in one corner, as far from the rest as was possible for her to be, with the children gathered around her: the youngest was very sick; the doctor had given up all hopes of its living; but it was still alive when we arrived in San Francisco.

An Irish lady, some eighty years old, started in company with her daughter, for California, as steerage passengers. She, being old and feeble, fell overboard in re-embarking at Greytown. What little baggage she possessed could not be had just then; consequently had to remain in her wet clothes, which brought on sickness. She lived to get on board the Moses Taylor; but died some seven or eight days after we left San Juan del Sur.

When I went around among the steerage passengers, and saw the fare and accommodations they I had, did not wonder a lady of her age should die for want of care, after the exposure she had passed through. She was coming to make her home with her son, living somewhere in California, but was committed to the deep as a last resting-place, in the usual form of a burial at sea.

Our passengers had, by this time, been together long enough to throw off all restraint and act in their natural dispositions, and many flirtations were going on, even among the married ladies. There was a gentleman of fifty married to a girl of sixteen: he was quite fine looking; the report on board was, she had, as a great many others have done, married him for his money, and did not act as though she cared much for him; she seemed to delight in tormenting him in every way she could; would steal away to have a chat with some nice young fop.

Whenever we would see the old gentleman coming around peering into every corner, and looking so nervous, we would know Anna had escaped. If you would see him sitting with his eyes fixed on the floor, looking like some melancholy lunatic, you might know he could not find his darling Anna, as he called her.

On one occasion she came on deck hanging on a man's arm, promenaded past her husband, as though she did not see him, went forward to the bow of the boat, turned and came back until she stood opposite, then sprung toward him. She said, "Why, Pa, what is the matter? You look as though you would jump overboard;" at same time looking up at the young man and winking; still I do not think she meant any harm, for I often overheard them talking, when he would be lecturing her severely; her replies were always something after this fashion: "Oh nonsense, I am going to to have a good time while I can, what's the use of being so pokey," and away she would go, humming some lively tune, such as "I am the girl that's gay and happy," &c. There were many other married ladies who were older and more experienced, that got into trouble; for them I had no sympathy. Altogether, we had a nice respectable crowd.

I often would amuse myself for hours watching the Mexican shore, and thought it looked very much like some great fire had passed over it all. I was told herds of cattle would keep fat among the hills and mountains, but *I* could not see how even a mountain goat could subsist, they looked so barren.

In *some* places were small cañons, where vegetation seemed to grow. Here and there the captain would point out some trail or road winding around the mountains.

One day he showed us, at some little distance, smoke, which he said was issuing from a volcano. In the evenieg as we drew nearer to it, a red light could be seen. We did not stop at Acapulco. But at Manzanillo the steamer rounded to. She was soon surrounded by natives with small boats, containing different varieties of tropical fruit for sale. It was amusing to watch the various modes they had of conveying the fruit on board.

Some had long ropes they would fling to the passengers, attached to some kind of a basket, and they would draw them on board. Other natives would throw oranges, limes, &c, on deck and seemed to be much pleased, by the broad grin on their faces, at our trying to catch them. Many pranks were played by some of our jolly chaps. Alabama, who had by this time got all right and at his tricks as usual, was standing on the lower deck with some gentleman's cane, and as the passengers on the upper deck were pulling up a basket of fruit, he would draw it to him with the hook end of the cane, and take the fruit out, which made the natives angry.

At this place, a Spaniard got on board, bound for San Francisco. It was said he had a large quantity of coffee with him for the market. A short time was passed at Manzanillo, which broke the monotony of the trip, the little boats pulled away toward the shore, and the steamer made preparations to leave. I watched the little boats and their dusky owners with great interest. In their dark, swarthy faces could plainly be seen a miniature of the African and Indian races. In their mouth and nose they resemble the African, and in their straight black hair, and snake-like eyes the Indian.

They wore loose shirts or blouses, pants fastened around the waist, with a red sash or broad belts, in which they carried long dirk-knives; all bare-footed and some bare-headed. They looked to me very savage and uncivilized.

My attention was drawn by my husband to a long train of pack mules, leaving the town and winding their way up the mountains. The scenery around this place was quite beautiful. The town itself was very small, the houses seemed to be built like those described heretofore at Greytown.

In crossing the Gulf of California, it was very rough.

I suffered with fear more than at any other time during the voyage.

The Moses Taylor rolled fearfully. A lady told me it was called the rolling Moses. I think she well deserved the name. Some of the passengers preferred the rolling of the steamer to the terrible pitching of the Guiding Star, but I liked it on the other side much better; by sitting in the centre of it, you could scarcely feel the motion, while on this one you could feel it no matter where you went.

It was very cold and foggy. The waves rolled high. I would stand and watch them as they arose, then fell with a dull roaring sound, sprinkling the guards with their spray.

It was a wild grand scene. It seemed to hold me spell-bound, while at the same time a great fear took possession of me. I hope I never may, as long as I live, experience the same feelings I had in crossing the Gulf of California.

The first point of land we saw was Cape San Lucas. It was very cold, and no one could venture on deck, without being well protected.

I left the guards, and went on the upper deck. Here I found Miss S., in company with an Englishman. The former clad in a long water-proof cloak, with the hood drawn over her head; looking pale, as though she had just come out of a fainting fit. I took a seat near them.

He was telling about his large ranch in California; his 'orses, carriages and servants; he said when she arrived there she could 'ave a fine 'orse, and as 'andsome a riding 'abit as could be found in the city. I think she believed every word he said, from the way she looked and acted. I guess Miss S. never enjoyed her ranch life, as I heard he was a bar-keeper in a low saloon, and hadn't a cent in the world. Some time after his arrival here he cut his throat.

Every day passed pretty much the same as its predecessor; once in a while some one would halloo, "A whale, a whale!" I would often run and look in the direction it was pointed out, but can say I never saw one. Sometimes I would see the water spirt up, and would be told it was a whale blowing; but I think *they* were only *blowing*.

I often caught sight of other different kinds of fish, and saw any amount of sea-gulls. They sometimes followed the steamer in large flocks. It was quite amusing to throw something into the water and see them all dive after it. Often some of the passengers would fire a pistol or a shot-gun among them, and if any were killed or wounded, the remainder would chirp and hover o'er them, as though mourning their loss.

On the evening of the 7th of May, at the supper-table, the news went around that this was our last meal on board the steamer. This was pleasant news to me, although I dreaded to pass through the Golden Gate. I had heard the first mate tell some of the passengers we would have a rough time of it, he expected. I inquired if it would be as rough as crossing the Gulf. He said, "Yes, much *worse*, for here we have to cross the bar."

I went to my state-room in great excitement, and thought of the little Active on the bar, in the Colorado River, and my fear in crossing the Gulf of California. In this way I passed the evening; then I lay down with my clothes on; after much worrying fell asleep, and awakened about daylight. I found my

husband up; he said he was going on deck to see them
pass through the Golden Gate. I went with him.

When I got there, and saw how near we were to the
entrance, I rushed back to my state-room with my little
girl, crawled into a berth, and made her follow my
example. I lay there trembling, thinking every minute
the steamer would be dashed to pieces, turn bottom
side up, or something else, I scarcely knew what;
still she moved along, if anything, smoother than ever.
In a short time, Mrs. F. came in, saying, "What on
earth are you doing here? Why ain't you out sight-seeing?"
I told her she had better come and lie
down, because we would cross the bar soon. When
she laughed loudly, saying, "Why, we have already
passed over it. You must get up and make preparations
to go ashore."

I soon turned out, and thought what a fool I had
made of myself; I went outside to look, as I could
hardly believe her, and found we were opposite the
Barracks.

The steamer seemed to be standing very still. I
noticed several United States officers on board, who,
in company with the Captain, visited every portion of
the vessel; some said they would not let us land, as
the measles were *yet* on board. I began to get Polly
ready to go on shore; taking her from her perch, I
once *again* put her in the basket, tied her up, and set
the basket down to wait their decision.

The steamer began to move once more. All on
board was bustle and confusion. I and my family
were busy in getting ready to land, our wide-brimed
Panama hats were laid aside for smaller and more
suitable ones; not wishing to discard them altogether,
I rolled them up, so as to carry them conveniently.

At last the word was given to go ashore; although we had a nice time and pleasant weather, I cannot say I am partial toward the water.

In hurrying to land I had forgotten all about the hats I had tied up; looking around to see if I had dropped them, I saw Alabama with them on a long stick, whirling them around, and singing to the tune of Susannah, the words, "O! California, you're the place for me, I'm now in California with the hat-rack on my knee," &c. but I did not stop to listen; taking my little girl by the hand I pushed my way through the crowd. We reached the American Exchange coach, where my husband and some of my fellow passengers were waiting.

CHAPTER IV.

San Francisco.

Being seated, we were driven to the hotel. As we passed up and down the streets, we looked around in hopes of getting some idea what kind of a place it was; and I must say I was somewhat disappointed with the view it presented, especially in the lower part of the city, but it gradually improved as we drew near the hotel.

The American Exchange is too well known on this coast to need any comments from me, but I *can* say, the few days I remained there, the table was supplied with the best the market afforded. The rooms were comfortable, and everything seemed to be done with care and neatness.

The next morning Mr. F. showed us around the city

We visited many places, among them the California market.

I have been in different markets, in several large cities, such as New Orleans, Mobile, St. Louis, Louisville, Cincinnati and others; none could compare with this for varieties, order and neatness, with the exception of one at Philadelphia; but I suppose I should not compare it with San Francisco, one a grand old city of many years, the other, in comparison, but a city of a day.

We next visited Woodward's Gardens; here I was much surprised to see such a large and fine collection of stuffed birds. We passed through all the buildings and around the grounds. I have seen many private and public cabinets, which contained choice selections from every portion of the globe, many museums, horticultural grounds and hot-houses; also, art galleries; I have stood in wonder at the beauties man could bring forth with pencil, brush and talent, still in this young city I find owned by Mr. Woodward as fine a variety for the amusement of the public as I have ever seen.

I left the Gardens murmuring many praises for his taste and energy.

The next morning, Mr. F. said he had made up his mind to settle in San José, and invited us to go and stop with them until we could look around, and make up *our* minds what we would do.

I gladly accepted the invitation, for I was now so homesick I could not bear the thought of being separated from my friend Mrs. F.

Four o'clock found us on our way to San José. After we had passed several stations, I began to think, from the looks of the country through which the cars passed, Santa Clara County might *well* be called the Garden Spot of California.

We arrived at San José just before dark, and stopped at a small hotel on First Street, called the Morgan House, where we were shown to neat and tidy rooms. After supper we collected in the parlor, where Mr. W., the landlord, and his wife, whom, by the way, we found very pleasant people, related to us their trip to California, the first house they lived in, and their many trials in getting started in business. Bidding them good evening, we went to our rooms, where we planned for the morrow. Mrs. F. and I concluded to rent a house together.

In the morning it was foggy and cold. After breakfast Mr. F. and my husband went to Mr. C's real estate office, and soon returned with the keys to several houses. We went around to see them, and finally rented one on Third Street. The balance of the day was spent in buying a few things necessary for housekeeping.

I did not wish to buy very much furniture, until we knew where we would settle.

Being worn out, we retired early; but very little sleep did we get that night, for the fleas nearly carried us away. I lay and thought of all the stories I had read concerning bed-bugs and fleas; one of them was about a teamster, who stopped over night at a country hotel; finding he could not sleep in the bed for the bed-bugs, he thought he would fix them: going out to his wagon, he got his blankets and a pail of tar; returning to the room, he spread the blankets on the floor, and made a ring of tar around them; he then laid down, thinking he would have a good sleep.

"But, by Jove," he said "if they did not crawl up the

wall and along the ceiling until they got right over me, and then fell."

I am afraid if I had the tar, and tried his experiment, those San José fleas would have jumped over it, they were so large and strong.

After passing a sleepless night, and eating a hasty breakfast, my husband started out in search of employment. He tried for several days, but each day would return home tired and pale, having found nothing his strength would permit him to do. This combined to make me still more homesick, and almost wish I had never come to California. It was Sunday morning; I and my family started out in search of the Methodist Episcopal church. Upon my husband inquiring for it, we were shown where it stood.

As I passed its threshold, a great change came over me. I was now in the house of God, in a strange land, and among strange people. A few moments after we were seated, the pastor in charge arose and commenced delivering his morning services.

I could *now* refer to the text, repeat much of his sermon and many words in his prayer, but I am not writing a religious work, and do not wish to mingle the sublime with the ridiculous.

I here remark, the sermon was excellent. After church was over, the minister came forward and introduced himself. It was the Rev. Mr. Dunn. Many of the members also came forward, and seemed to give us a hearty welcome. In the afternoon we attended the Sunday-School; found it well conducted under the superintendence of Mr. Clayton.

During the following week, my husband went to San Francisco, to see if he could get a position at either of the railroad offices. He called on H. M. N., who promised to see the Superintendent and try to get him a situation, and let him know in a few days. When my husband returned to San José he seemed in better spirits.

Two days passed in suspense, then a dispatch came from Mr. ———, the Assistant Superintendent, for my husband to report in San Francisco immediately. He was off by the first train.

For several days I heard nothing from him, when a letter came saying he had a situation of overseeing the freight shipped on the passenger trains in connection with the baggage, and wished me to come to San Francisco. Enclosed I found passes for myself and child.

I here return my thanks to H. M. N ——— and Mr. H———, for their many kindnesses shown my husband.

When I arrived in the City I found him looking much better. He was boarding and lodging at a restaurant at the San José Depot, on Market street. He took us to his room. As we passed up the narrow, rough, uncarpeted stairs, through the dark hall, the gloomy appearance of everything made me almost shudder. I found the room plainly but neatly furnished, with two large windows looking out on the platform of the depot.

At the supper table I was introduced to the landlord and lady, also to a gentleman and his wife who were boarding, whom I will call Mr. and Mrs. T———. I could not keep my eyes off the latter; she looked so sad and heart-broken I pitied her. This is Sunday, but I did not attend church, as my husband had to work.

Monday morning I started out house-hunting. I soon secured one.

Tuesday I returned to San José, packed my furniture, had it conveyed to the depot, and shipped to San Francisco. In a few days I was nicely settled in the City, and everything went on smoothly until the eighteenth night in July.

About midnight my daughter was awakened by the screeching of the parrot, to find the house filled with smoke. She had some difficulty in awakening my husband and me, as we were almost smothered by the smoke.

As we hurried down the stairs, everything was aglare. We saw Polly crouching at the foot, where in fright she had flown from her perch. We picked her up, and escaped into the street, just as the flames rushed into the hall.

Our furniture and clothing were totally destroyed by either fire or water. I afterward learned the fire originated from a defective flue. A kind neighbor gave us lodgings for the night. In the morning we went over to the same restaurant, where we procured board and lodgings. This room was not so nice as the first one we had, being dark and small, but it was *cheaper*. I knew I must be very saving, for our money was *almost* gone. My husband had taken cold and felt much worse. Here I will drop the curtain for awhile over the scene.

CHAPTER V.

August 11th, 1868.

Now begins the one great struggle of my life. I scarcely know where to turn or what to do. As I look around the room, I see nothing but want and poverty on every hand. Something must be done to get out of this place. Bidding my dear ones keep up courage, I start out. Never before did I know the meaning of the word poverty. Now I felt it in all its keenest pangs—everything looked dark and cloudy. I started for the Post-office. Not being able to pay car hire, I went on foot. On my way I passed the book-store of H. H. Bancroft, then on the corner of Montgomery and Merchant streets. In the window I noticed a card, with the words "Agents Wanted" on it. Stepping into the store a gentlemen advanced to meet me. I asked him "Do you employ ladies agents?" "Yes", he replied, " allow me to take you to the Subscription Department." There I was shown to the gentleman in charge. I found him to be a frank kind-hearted gentleman. Will I ever forget him, for it was he who cheered me with his pleasant words. After talking for a few moments, he showed me an engraving of Grant and his Family, in upright form; told me his terms, what to sell it for, and how much commission I would get. Knowing as I did that something must be done by me, we made a bargain; he giving me a book to take orders in, and two of the pictures, told me to go on Montgomery street. I left the store with more elastic steps than I had since my arrival in California. I started up the street, but did not have the courage to stop until I reached Mr. M., on Washington street; he bought the two and gave me the coin for them. How I thanked him; I think if he had refused, I should not have had courage enough to ask any one else. I hastened back to the store, paid Mr. S. for them, and had four more rolled up for me. It was now three hours since I had left home.

Taking them on my arm, order-book in my hand, I started up Montgomery street, calling on one and all, up stairs and down, in every room.

Some looked at me curiously, others with pity, and *some few* with contempt, while I endeavored, in my embarrassment, and in an awkward way, to show the picture.

I worked on faithfully until three o'clock in the afternoon, when I returned to my miserable room; but it contained those dear to me, where I found them very anxious about me. They soon cheered up, as I told them the events of the day.

Tuesday morning I again resumed my work; for five days I canvassed steadily, nothing of importance occurring.

In this time I made many dollars, which I put to good use, buying comforts for myself and family, and preparing my little girl for school again.

Eight o'clock every morning would find me in the street-car on my way to the business part of the city. I had one of the pictures mounted on canvass and rollers, that I used as a sample copy, taking orders, to be delivered in two or three weeks, and sometimes as far as two months.

It was now just before Grant's election, and great excitement concerning it prevailed. The Democrats arguing in favor of *their* candidate, and the Republicans in favor of *theirs*.

In almost *every* room, in front of every store or business house, and on every street corner, I would find gentlemen in groups, whispering or conversing in low tones; I suppose plotting and planning for the coming campaign; while others were loud and boisterous in expressing their opinions.

It was a great trial for me to know just how to approach them, for the one almost frightened me, and the others so grave and solemn, still I did not pass any of them; with a heavy heart I would step up, unroll the picture, saying, "Gentlemen, I have a fine engraving of General Grant and his family."

After they had looked at it, which they very seldom failed to do, I would present my order-book, take them in rotation, and insist upon one and all to subscribe, and was generally very successful. They would treat me kindly, and were very polite, with the exception of some few ruffians who seemed to have forgotten "their mother was a woman," would hurt my feelings, in many ways, with regards to Grant's life and character, on this coast, before the war; as though *I* was accountable for the way he had acted.

I will here relate a circumstance. I went into a lawyer's office on Montgomery street. It was richly furnished, with care and neatness. At a table were seated two young gentlemen; at a desk was seated a person whom I took to be a gentleman, from the looks of his back.

When I spoke to the young gentleman concerning the picture, he whirled around in the chair, and, oh, horrors, what a repulsive face. I *had never* seen any thing to equal it.

With a snarl, and the authority of a king, he said, "I don't want you to bother those boys, woman; what is it you want? I will attend to you." I politely showed him the picture. He looked up, with his blinky eyes, and crooked mouth, in which there was an attempt to grin. "I would buy the engraving if it had his squaw wife and Indian babies on it; we cannot trade madam," and he turned around to his desk.

I left the office, without daring to again ask the young gentlemen to buy; but as I passed them, and although they were busily writing, their faces showed they were deeply mortified.

When once alone in the hall, I sat down on the bottom stair that led to the third story of the building, and had a good cry.

Many passed me, looking at me wonderingly, but none addressed me. I dried my tears away, drew down my vail, and passed into the street. I had canvassed California street on both sides, from Front to Montgomery; on Montgomery, from California to Washington, and now made up my mind to try Front street, as Mr. S. had told me he *thought* I would be very successful there. I started in at California street, passed down the lower side to Washington.

The gentlemen whom I met were all pleasant and jolly. Democrats joking Republicans by saying, "Don't back out *now;* if the lady had a picture of Seymour *we* would buy it." Others would say, "Don't let him off, madam; he is as black as ever was." After many more jokes I passed up the other side.

Here I met a gentleman from the country, who was trading at one of the wholesale houses; he seemed very angry to think a woman should be selling pictures among so many men. He said I looked old enough to be married and have a family, and ought to be at home taking care of them.

I told him I knew I looked old, but he need not remind me of it; that I *had* a family and was trying to make an honest living for them, at the same time telling him I presumed he was a bachelor, who would not know how to appreciate a wife if he had one.

The proprietor laughed heartily, and said, "Madam, you guessed right." As I was wasting time I left him.

When I got to California street, my order-book showed fifty-three names I had taken on Front street. I next tried Davis street and took more orders than on any street of its size in the City. After this I took the rest of the business streets in rotation, canvassing them thoroughly, walking all day, and running the sewing-machine until late at night. I kept this up for six weeks, and was now canvassing on Third street, not succeeding very well.

An old man was standing in the door-way of his shop; I spoke to him, unrolled the picture and asked him to subscribe. He was a strong Democrat and was not long in letting me know it.

"You d—— women think you will rule the country. There is a clique of you who go prowling around, having secret meetings, lecturing all over the country on women's rights; *here you* are roaming around with that d— picture of that loafer Grant. There was one of your *clique* in here the other day, lecturing on temperance. I told her in plain English to leave my shop; I would have no women's rights around me."

I replied, " Thank you for your hint; I am not in your shop, nor do not intend crossing your door-way, for fear I might become polluted, for you certainly are the most profane ruffian I ever met."

At this he became very angry, and I *think* he would have struck me, *had he* dared. I passed on and canvassed for several blocks; all the gentlemen were polite and kind, until I came to Mr. B—e's large grocery store. Inside were a large crowd of gentlemen talking politics, some of them seemed very much excited.

I stepped inside, unrolled the engraving and held it up for inspection, but did not say a word. One redfaced half drunken fellow stepped up and with many airs took hold of the engraving, examined it for a minute and said: "This picture is very imperfect." "In what respect," I asked. He replied, "It has not Grant's Indian babies." I told him it was better to be father of Indian babies than, like Seymour, not the father of any."

At this they laughed loudly. I looked at them for a second before I thought what I had said. I hurried away without asking any to subscribe. One of the gentlemen came out and called to me. I went back and four of them subscribed.

Next day I tried Kearny street, and took many orders, before I reached the City Hall; here I turned down Merchant street, until I came to the lowest story of the building, determined to take the officers in rotation. I found Mr. B— behind the counter, who was very kind. After examining the engraving for some time he took my order-book, and signed his name. There were a great many of the street contractors in the office, among which he secured me some eight or ten names.

He returned to where I was standing, and showed me what he had done. I did not wish to take the money, as I could not deliver the pictures to them for two weeks. "Take it along," he said, "if you are mean enough to run away with so small a sum the country is well rid of you." Thanking them for their kindness I visited every room in the building. By the time I reached Washington street, I had twenty names on my order-book taken in the City Hall.

That evening, when I returned to the restaurant, I went to Mrs. T.'s room, (whom I have mentioned in another chapter.) After telling her how well I was succeeding, I tried to persuade her to take Sacramento, and some of the upper counties, also telling her I had contracted with Bancrofts for the whole Pacific Coast for the upright picture of the Grant family, in connection with many others.

It was some days before she would give me any definite answer concerning it, though finally consented to try and canvass Sacramento; for she, like myself, was very tired of the restaurant, and was willing to do anything that was honorable and honest to get away from it.

She went in company with me to the store, where I introduced her to Mr. S.; at first, she was somewhat embarrassed, but his kind and easy manners soon reassured her.

I told him I did not wish the whole Coast. That Mrs. T. could have Sacramento, Marysville and Grass Valley. The bargain was closed.

I now selected out of the remaining territory what I desired, which were San Francisco, Santa Clara and San Joaquin counties.

It was two months since I first began to canvass, and I had several hundred names, also had the money for many small engravings. Bancrofts were looking daily for a new supply from New York. I had made up my mind to go to San José to canvass and take orders, during the Fair in that place, which was to commence in a few days.

The afternoon before the opening of the Fair found me in a railway car, bound for San José. I thought how lonely it would be there in not finding my friend, Mrs. F., as they had gone to San Diego.

Although I had passed over the road four times previous to this, I could see new beauties in almost everything. In fact, in the former times, I was so home-sick I scarcely noticed anything. But the prospects looked much brighter to me now.

As I sat and gazed from the car-window, I could but compare the autumn here with that in the East. There, at this season of the year, I have often wandered through the woods, looked with admiration at the leaves, with their many tints, listened to the soft, low murmuring of the wind, while in the distance I heard the notes of some merry bird, keeping time with the sad rustling of the leaves beneath my feet, while here before me lies the Coast Range, sunburnt and barren in its uneven appearance, looking as though some great convulsion of the earth had thrown it there. This scene is both grand and sad, while the thoughts of the other are sublime.

We pass on, and are soon at San Mateo. The town is not very striking in its appearance. But the country on either side, as far as the eye can look, seems fine and well cultivated. The next place that takes my attention is Belmont. Off to the right is a winding cañon skirted with heavy timber, making it look very beautiful to me.

As we pass through Redwood City, I was told it was the county seat of San Mateo county; it seemed to be quite a lively and flourishing little town.

. There is Fair Oaks and Menlo Park, which are beautiful places for private residences.

At Santa Clara I did not get a view of the town, as it lies at some distance from the depot.

CHAPTER VI.

San Jose.

When I arrived at San José, I directed a hackman to take me to the Morgan House. The landlord recognized me at once, and seemed very glad to see me, but said he hadn't a vacant room in the house and recommended me to Mrs. M— on Third street.

At Mrs. M— I was shown to a nicely furnished room. When the bell rang for dinner I descended to the dining-room. At the table were several ladies and gentlemen; all strangers to me. The landlady inquired my name and introduced me to all.

The meal passed pleasantly. I found them to be polite and genteel in manners and appearances.

Next morning I went to the hall where the Fair was to be held, to try and secure some space where I might put a small table and a chair, but there wasn't any vacancy. The agent for the Florence Sewing Machine, who had a large space, kindly offered me room in one corner. Mrs. M— the landlady, loaned me a table and a chair. After they were conveyed to the hall, I arranged my pictures on the table and took my seat behind them, feeling more like a culprit than anything else.

Although it was a short time since I had commenced

to canvass, and knew it was an honorable and legitimate business, still it *seemed* to me very much like begging. As ladies and gentlemen would pass me, I would try in many ways to gain their attention, but I acted so awkward and out of place that I did not succeed very well.

Some would stop for a moment and admire the engraving; few ladies would insist upon their husbands buying, but I scarcely took any orders.

I soon found it was not the place for me; if I wish to sell anything I must get out among the crowd.

Standing close to the entrance, I tackled every one I would see, something after the fashion of a little news-boy.

"Ladies and gentlemen, here's a fine engraving of General Grant and family," insisting upon one and all, who stopped to look at it for a moment, to subscribe. In the afternoon as I was going around among the machinery, I overheard an old man, who had a patent wash-boiler, "and I suppose feeling very important," say to one of the superintendents of the Fair, as he passed by him, "Why do you allow that woman around here with that picture, trying to get everyone's attention; why, a minute ago, while a gentleman was looking at the boiler, she had the impudence to ask him to patronize her."

He answered, "This is a free country, and as she don't seem to be doing any harm, she has as much right in here as any one else." At this the patent boiler man seemed to become a little embarrassed, but made no reply. In the evening I attended the Fair as a spectator, not as peddler.

I could not help but notice everything was arranged with good taste. I think there were the finest and largest apples, pears and grapes I ever saw. The canned fruit and jellies, in glass jars and tumblers, looked very inviting.

I stopped to examine the needle-work, wax-flowers, and paintings. The most interesting of all to me was the silk worms. I listened to the man in charge, while he explained their habits and customs, and could not help looking on them with curiosity, to think that mulberry leaves could be converted into material for our finest silk fabrics through the agency of these homely-looking worms.

The next day I went around to the Court House. The officers were all very kind and polite. I received several orders. During the day I visited many offices and stores; being very successful, Mrs. M., the landlady, told me in the evening she thought I would do well to go to the Fair that night and take my picture. I did so, and had quite good success, taking orders for several of "Lincoln and Family," "Washington and Family," also of the "Grant Family," saying they wished a group of the three great men of the United States. In the evening, I heard some one talking about a gentleman who had small photographs of different varieties, and a book written by himself. I inquired whether he was in the hall, and was told he had a small space at the far end of the building. I concluded to go and see him; when I came quite close to him the thought struck me to stand and watch *his* manner of doing *the* business.

He was standing, with his books and pictures lying on an oval table in front of him; they were arranged neatly, and showed well. I listened to his fast talk in recommending his goods; my thoughts were, "I'll have no chance while this gentleman's around."

I stepped up to his table; he turned politely and commenced urging me to buy. I told him I did not wish to purchase, as I was in the same occupation. I told him, upon inquiry, what subject I had. He said he had seen the engraving; it was very fine, and hoped I would be successful. I thanked him and wished him the same. I learned afterward his name was D—.

When I returned to my seat again, I found one of the ladies who had charge of the sewing-machines trying her best to sell one of the pictures. I helped her to close the bargain, and thanked her very much for the interest she had taken. It being late, I returned to the boarding-house, well pleased with my day's labor.

I continued my work there for several days longer, then returned to San Francisco; next day, after my arrival, I went down to Bancroft's. I showed Mr. S. my order-book, with which he seemed to be well pleased, saying, "You have done splendid." I thought so, too, as I had taken sixty orders during my absence. He told me the engravings of the Grant family had come, and I could commence delivering that day if I wished; counting out as many as I could conveniently carry, I left the store and went up Montgomery street. Using my order-book for a guide, I called on each one in succession who had subscribed; they all treated me kindly, taking their engraving, and some gave me orders for frames, on which I also made quite a good commission.

In this way, I worked very hard all day; as fast as one lot was delivered, would return to the store for a fresh supply. I now began to realize that taking orders for pictures, and delivering them were quite different things, the latter being very laborious.

I continued to work for several days, as I was in much need of the commission I was to get on them. At the same time, felt anxious to deliver as many as possible each day, so that my employers should have no cause of complaint.

I now began to think about looking up a house, so that we might go to house-keeping again. After some difficulty, I procured rooms on Fourth street, near Howard.

This morning I had concluded to go down into the City and buy some furniture, for the purpose of fitting up my rooms. I had just got my little girl ready for school, and about to put on *my* hat and shawl to start on my errand, when the *house commenced* rocking and shaking at an alarming rate; my little girl said, "Mamma, what is the matter?"

The cars never shook the house so before. The Polly was flying around in her cage, and seemed very much frightened. I did not realize myself what it was, until the second shock, then I exclaimed "Oh, this must be an earthquake, let us run into the street." We started, she gathering the cage in her hand containing the Polly. As we passed through the hall, I heard the whatnot fall in the ladies' parlor, breaking the vases and other things on it, and making quite a noise. Before we got clear of the house, an old wardrobe standing in the hall fell behind us with a great crash; then I thought *surely* the *house* was coming down on our heads, and expected every instant to be crushed to death.

But amid all the danger and confusion, as I passed through the hall by the landlady's room-door, I could not help noticing her, lying full length on the floor throwing her hands wildly about, exclaiming, "Oh

Lord, save us, Oh Lord, save us," at the top of her voice.

When we reached the street, the sidewalk seemed to be still moving. We hurried down the platform toward the baggage-room in search of my husband, who had gone there but a few moments before. I found him standing in the door-way laughing. I said, "How can you laugh at anything so terrible as this?" He replied, he "could not help laughing to see those piles of lumber in front of the office dancing;" also said, "that as far as that was concerned, if the earthquake was going to sink the City, he did not see why we might not as well go down laughing as crying, as crying would not save us."

Many gentlemen came into the office laughing, talking and jesting about the earthquake, which seemed to me to be perfect mockery, for from my feelings then, I thought at every shock we should all be swallowed up.

I often smile now to myself when I think how ridiculous I must have appeared that morning, running down the platform with my hat in my hand, my shawl dragging, and almost crying; my little girl closely folfowing. dragging after her the large cage with the Polly in it.

I stayed around the platform all day, and no one could persuade me to go into the house, until night drove me there. *Then* I lay down with all my clothes on, ready to run at any moment, and wished myself back in Ohio a thousand and one times.

It was two days before I could get up sufficient courage to venture up into the City to commence work again. I selected furniture for our rooms, and moved what few traps we had at the restaurant, and *once more* commenced house-keeping. Everything passed off pleasantly for two weeks, with plenty of work and liberal patronage.

CHAPTER VII.

I now concluded to go to Santa Clara and canvass that town, before delivering my pictures in San José. Eight o'clock in the evening found me seated in the ladies' parlor at the hotel, conversing with the landlord concerning the severe shock of earthquake we had two weeks previous.

He explained to me how the sliding iron doors of the hotel had come together, and he thought had shut them in at first, but as the convulsion of the earth continued, they opened again, and allowed the inmates to pass out into the street, which they were not long in doing. The shock was so severe, that they had apprehensions the house would fall before they could escape.

After conversing awhile on different subjects, he bade me good evening and went below. As I passed through the hall on the way to my room, noticed the ceiling was bare in some places where the plastering had fallen off; the walls were badly cracked. Taking a light from the stand, I went into my room almost fearing to lock the door, lest another shock might come, and I could not escape.

I thought, if the Lord spared me, I would not stay another night in a brick house. I had partially undressed when the house commenced shaking. Frightened

EARTHQUAKE SCENE AT SANTA CLARA, CAL.

all but to death, I scarcely knew what to do; but found myself in the door-way with the candle in my hand, thinking I must not go into the street in this condition. There came a second shock. I blew out the light, threw it on the floor, and rushed into the street, not caring how I appeared. It was full of people. Some of them looked at me curiously; but I drew my shawl close about me and stood my ground, nor could I be persuaded to return to my room. The clerk brought me my shoes and baggage, and took me where he knew I could obtain lodgings, to a lady's, a few doors away. She gladly offered me shelter, as her husband was away from home, and she was very lonely.

There were several light shocks after I had been there. Next morning, many joked me about my appearance the evening previous, especially Mr. W., who said he never would forget how comical and frightened I looked.

During the day I took several orders, sold a great many and received the coin for them. I had taken some eleven or twelve to Santa Clara with me. I made arrangements to stay with the lady until I should leave town, so I went back and spent the night.

After breakfast, I started for Mrs. W's., who lived a half or three-quarters of a mile from town. I found her and husband living on a fruit ranch. She did not recognize me at first.

I told her I had brought the picture she had subscribed for one evening, at the Fair in San José. She remembered it, took the Grant picture, and gave me an order for the engravings of Washington and Lincoln's families. She gave me some choice pears, grapes, and a *piece of pie*, insisting upon my eating them, as she said I looked very tired. Everything in and around the house, so far as I could see, showed a neat and tidy housewife. I promised to bring the engravings in a short time, also thanked her for her kindness, and returned to Santa Clara.

After lunch I started out along the Alameda, toward San José. I had sold all the engravings I had brought with me, so I made up my mind to call at every house and take orders, to be delivered in two weeks. The houses were very scattering, and I found it slow and tiresome work; but I enjoyed walking in the shade of those stately old trees that line either side of that favorite resort of San José and Santa Clara for driving. It reminded me of portions of Bourbon County, Kentucky. In that county is *one* of the dearest spots on earth to me, for it was my childhood home. I came to the place where they were about to establish the depot of the Santa Clara and San José street railroad. Here were several gentlemen collected. Among them was one without a coat, who did not seem to be working very hard, although the perspiration was streaming down his face. I did not wonder at it, he was so large and fleshy; he reminded me of the darkey song, "he's tree foot one way, six foot tudder, and weighs tree hundred pounds," and as for his coat, it was nowhere around.

However, I ventured up and addressed him, unrolled the engraving for his inspection; he looked up, politely bowed, viewed it for some time, occasionally wiping the perspiration from his face with his hand.

Turning his head to one side he laughed jovially, and said, "Old Grant is no favorite of mine; but if you will bring me a good engraving of his Indian family I will buy it. Will you?" I replied, "The demand for such an engraving seems so great I certainly shall order some for the accommodation of people of such refined taste."

Then the three hundred pounds looked at me sharply, as much as to say, "I don't sabé," but I kept a very grave look on my face, and said, "I shall most assuredly bring you a picture of the kind you desire, and shall expect you to take it off my hands."

I showed the engraving to a number of other gentlemen standing around, and insisted upon their buying it, but did not get a single order.

I bid them good day, and took up my line of march toward San José. It was now getting late, so I did not stop at any more houses, but hurried on, until I reached the Morgan House, on First street; here I partook of a light supper, went to my room very tired, having walked about six miles during the day.

Next morning I arose not much refreshed, partook a hasty breakfast, and visited the Express Office; found my package of engravings all right; had them sent up to the hotel, where I soon followed.

I found Bancroft's had also sent a number of small engravings on different subjects. Taking an armful of the Grant pictures, I started out to fill my orders in this place.

I worked very hard for several days, and with good success, selling a great many small ones, and taking orders for Grant, Lincoln, and Washington families. I had now canvassed the business part of the town thoroughly, and made up my mind to try what success I would have among the private families. Many ladies had been recommended to me, as being very liberal, and believed in patronizing their own sex; so I concluded to make one of them my first victim.

She lived several blocks from the business part of

the town; while on my way I had plenty of time for reflecting, and wondered how I should be received, as this was my first effort to canvass among the ladies.

My somewhat long walk brought me in front of the residence of my intended first victim, who was the dashing widow of the lately deceased Mr.——, as I shall call her. I opened the gate and passed in through the neatly laid out and well-kept grounds.

I passed up to the front door, and timidly pulled the bell, and waited for the appearance of the servant, or I thought, maybe the lady herself might appear to admit me, and perhaps might invite me into her parlor, and might even go so far as ask me to stay for tea, as it was getting late in the afternoon.

After waiting sometime, with as much bashfulness as a young miss of sixteen awaiting her first beau, the door opened just sufficient for the dashing widow to see who the intruder was; instead of the cordial handshaking and hearty welcome I had expected, while awaiting her appearance the first words that greeted my ears were, "What is wanted, Madam?" at the same time holding a tight grip on the door, I suppose lest I might burst it open, rush past her and take the castle by storm. I had no such intentions, but politely told her I had a very fine engraving of General Grant and family; would like her to look at it, and perhaps could induce her to buy.

She said she had no use for such things and had no money to fool away for such purposes; still keeping her hold on the door, which was so nearly closed I did not get a full view of her august person. This liberal lady, I learned, was a leading member of one of the fashionable churches, and gave quite freely of her wealth, whenever an opportunity offered for it to be proclaimed publicly that the dashing widow had given hundreds for such, and such, a charitable purpose.

I had always been used to civil treatment from my own sex at least, and turned away with disgust *from this*, what the world calls a *liberal lady*, and must confess with scarcely sufficient courage left to call on another of the same liberal reputation.

When I reached Mrs. J— I concluded to go in. She also was a descendant of the same family, but I found her very different, treating me kindly and politely, conducting me into the parlor, and inviting me to rest myself, while she examined the engravings. After looking them all over, she stepped into another room, and brought out an engraving of the Grant family, which her husband had purchased of me a few days previous.

We conversed awhile, then thanking her for her kindness I bid her good afternoon.

As I passed down the street, I saw a new and neat house, and inquired of a boy, who lived there; was told by him Mrs. C—, whose husband was a buyer of grain. I went up the steps and rang the bell; it was answered by Mrs. C—, in person; she is very nice looking, well dressed and a perfect lady in her manners, she cordially invited me in, and with her easy conversation made me feel quite at home. She examined the engravings and purchased two of the smaller ones. It was late and I returned to the hotel, concluding to take a new start next day.

In the morning I set out for Gen. N—'s residence; this I found at quite a distance, but did not mind it much for the morning was pleasant, and the air balmy.

When I reached the gate that led into his grounds, it was just nine o'clock. As I passed through the wide winding carriage-drive, thickly skirted on both sides with evergreens and ornamental trees, it looked dark and gloomy. I did not see his cottage until I was right upon it. The appearance of the dwelling outside is not in keeping with his grounds.

After rapping at several of the doors, I did not find any one at home. I looked around me; saw at a distance the gardener; in answer to my inquiry, he told me the General and family were away. I asked his permission to go over the grounds, which he readily granted, thanking him, I started down the wide foot-path, bordered with flowers, and small shrubs of the choicest variety; now and then a tree thickly entwined with creeping vines.

Sometimes I would see a narrow path leading off to the left, so thickly covered overhead with honeysuckle, making the entrance so low, I would have to stoop to see where it led A few yards away was a neat small summer-house, dark and gloomy looking as though it might be a romantic lover's retreat. I wandered on, passed over a rustic foot-bridge that spanned a small stream, while overhead were large weeping willows, their branches dipping in the water beneath.

I stepped back upon the bridge, for the spot seemed delightful, although gloomy. To the left was a small grove of weeping willows, while around and about them were many rustic seats.

In front of them, on an elevation was a small artificial lake, supplied by a flowing well, the waste water forming the stream beneath my feet.

The wide path through which I had just come led to the hot-houses. I did not visit them, as my time was limited. Turning to the left, I passed around the lake, watched the numerous fishes playing in its waters, passed down the stone steps into the same dark drive I had first entered, out through the gate, and was once more on Santa Clara street.

I now went out to Tenth street, down Tenth until I came to Mrs. Dr. S——'s, whose husband raised fruit. I had met them one evening at the Fair, and promised to call at their residence. I inquired of a small boy, who pointed out the house. They have a beautiful place. At the edges of the sidewalk around the grounds was planted maples, which are now large and stately trees. I noticed the yard was tastefully laid out; there were many choice flowers and shrubs. I crossed the porch and rung the bell.

Mrs. S— answered the bell, recognized me, invited me in, bought three different engravings, and sent for her married daughter, who lived next door, to come and examine them.

Mrs. F—, the daughter, purchased a few. They invited me to stay for lunch, which I gratefully accepted, as I wished to canvass that portion of the town in the afternoon. After lunch, thanking them for their hospitality, I started out, calling at every house in rotation. I was treated kindly and politely, and found the ladies very liberal.

It was almost dark when I reached the hotel. In the morning I went in the direction of the San José Institute. It was quite cold; by the time I reached Mrs. W— I was chilled through. She invited me into a neat sitting-room where there was a bright fire.

Although she was a *widow* and a lady of considerable wealth, she *condescended* to treat *me*, a *canvasser*, with respect, and gave me her patronage, also a pair of warm gloves.

Calling at several houses, and being in the vicinity of Judge D—'s residence, I concluded to call and fulfill his order, given to me a few days previous, for a picture of General Grant and family.

His married daughter was sitting on the porch; she asked me to be seated while I told her my errand. She called her father, who came out, accompanied by his wife and youngest daughter. He took the engraving. I found him and his daughters polite, but I must say his wife was rather abrupt in her manners.

During the day I called on Mrs. C—, whose husband is a house-painter. A little girl of six or seven years answered the bell, a timid and very delicate looking child. I stepped inside; Mrs. C— came forward and offered me a chair. She took the roll of engravings and spread them out upon the table, telling her little girl to select two, as she would buy them for her.

All the while they were examining them, I could not keep my eyes from Mrs. C—; clad in a dark muslin dress, with a spotless linen collar, she looked more stylish than many others in the finest of fabrics. Though not strikingly handsome, still in every line of her features could be seen a true and noble woman.

She looked like one who, if you could once gain her friendship, would be firm and steadfast; one who had a mind and will all her own, not ready to change with the slightest breeze. If the rough winds of adversity should sweep over you, sunshiny friends turn away, she would stand by you, and do all in her power ot shield you from its *second* blast.

I have tried her, and now know I was not deceived. But to my subject. The little miss selected two of the engravings; thanking her, I hurried away, as I wished to see Mr. P— before the bank closed. I had a slight acquaintaince with him during the short time we resided in San José. He recognized me, and gave me an order for an engraving. I returned to the hotel, where I remained for the balance of the day.

CHAPTER VIII.
Gilroy.

Next morning I took passage in the stage for Gilroy. The railroad was not completed any farther than San José at that time.

There were several gentlemen in the stage; one of them bound for Hollister, where he had purchased a ranch. I was very much amused at his description of the fertile and rich soil in and about Hollister. "Why," said he, "anything in the world will grow there. Mr. H., that I purchased the ranch of, would always raise three large cabbage-heads from one stalk; also, said he raised a sweet potato, so large that the family of five made a good meal off of it, and *all* of them were very fond of sweet potatoes. He also raised a beet that was so large the first season he concluded to let it stand for two or three more; until it grew so far out of the ground the wind broke it off, and it measured four feet across." That must have been a *dead beat*.

Near the Eighteen Mile House I saw a large flock of sheep, tended by a herder. When I first caught sight of them they were some distance away, feeding on an open plain, beyond a strip of woods.

I inquired of *dead beat* what that was growing off to the left, pointing in that direction; he said he did not see anything growing; just then I saw them moving, and observed what they were; by this time all the rest of the passengers were looking at them. I acknowledged myself sold, and joined in their merry laughter.

We passed over several tracts of land covered with timber, among which were many live oaks, some of them very large and beautiful, with their wide-spreading branches covered with thick foliage, looking as though they might be a safe retreat for man or beast, and would protect them from a heavy fall of rain.

We crossed the creek, and followed it for some little distance. The country around Gilroy seemed low and flat, as though it might be easily undulated in the rainy season. When we entered the town, I was surprised to see so small a place; but there were many new buildings going up, among them the Williams House; everything appeared brisk and lively. At this time there was but one hotel in the place. The stage drove up to the door.

It was a long, rough building, with several live oaks in front, which made it look much more inviting than it would otherwise have done. I was shown into a room they called the parlor. It was very poorly furnished; but on the hearth a bright fire was blazing, which made the room have a cheerful appearance.

In a corner were seated two ladies. I was not long in discovering they were Southern people. The youngest was trying to get the village school; the elderly lady, her mother, was very communicative, and gave me her whole history in a short time.

I sat and listened to her, and thought she would make a splendid agent, for she was such a fast talker in her way. She tried to find out my business in Gilroy, but I did not give her any satisfaction. She would look at me sharply when I avoided her questions, and finally turned to her daughter, saying, "Sal, that poor critter is to be pitied, for she is *mighty* deaf, and not got much *larning*, no how."

She then crossed the room to the table, where I had laid my engravings, picked up the sample copy, took it close to the window, and put it to her eyes, as though she thought it was an opera glass, unrolled it, saying, "Humph! picture, hey?" came to where I was sitting, held it up before me, screamed in my ear, until it made me jump, "Peddling, I reckon." I looked at her in amazement, but made no reply.

She returned to the window, saying, "That's mighty queer how *she* peddles; Sal, what's that thare reading?" Sal took the engraving, looked at the name on the bottom, spelled it over two or three times, and finally drawled out, "Why, it's old Grant and family, the darned old thief." I thought to myself, you would make a splendid school-marm.

The old lady stormed and capered around the room in such a manner, that I thought it time to interfere, for I was afraid she would tear the sample copy to pieces. She, at first, refused to give it to me, saying she "would burn the darned thing up." I told her it was not mine, that I was taking orders for Bancroft and Company; also, told her I, too, was a Southern woman, in reduced circumstances, and had to work for a living. She replied, "No, you ain't, you're a darned Yank, an impostor. There ware a heap on you going round in the Southern States, before the war, 'tending to peddle, all the time stealing nigs." She came close to me again, shaking her head, "I know you ain't much, else you wouldn't played deaf."

I replied, "Madam, you are mistaken; I did not say I was deaf, nor act as though I was. I did not wish to answer your numerous questions, nor treat you impolitely, so I did not say anything."

At this, she stormed at me in such a rough and unladylike manner, I think it best not to repeat what she said. I had intended not to go to my room until bedtime, for the evening was cold, and the warm fire felt very comfortable; but I could not endure her abuse, so I gathered up my traps and started for my room, laughing at her as I went, which seemed to enrage her still more.

When I entered the room, I locked and bolted the door, for fear she might follow me. When I awakened next morning, I heard the rain, as I thought, dripping from the branches of the trees on the roof of the house. The thoughts of having to wade around in the mud during the day made me feel anything but comfortable. I arose and went to the window, and was much relieved to find it nothing more than a heavy fog.

After breakfast, I commenced to canvass, calling at every house. I found it to be a lively and bustling town, the citizens kind and very benevolent, giving me a liberal patronage. In the afternoon I called at the pastor's residence of the M. E. Church. There I met a lady from Marion County, Ohio, who was well acquainted with my father-in-law and family. She had been in California for many years, and lived on a ranch close to old Gilroy. We had a pleasant chat for some time. I promised to call and see her if I ever happened to be in that part of the country again. Bidding her good afternoon, I returned to the hotel.

In the evening I made inquiries concerning my *Southern friends*, and was told they had returned to their ranch, some fifteen miles from Gilroy. The accomplished young lady was not successful in getting the school.

Next morning, early, found me in the stage, on my way for San José. Upon arriving there I took the cars for Mayfield. It is a small village in Santa Clara county, on the line of the railroad.

As I went down the street, towards the hotel, many looked at me wonderingly, and then at the large, long roll of engravings I carried in my arms. I did not address any of them.

When I looked around me, I saw many neat dwellings, with well laid-out grounds, which looked cosy and home-like. When I reached the hotel, the landlady showed me into a neat, comfortable room. She seemed to be a jolly, kind-hearted woman, full of fun and quite witty. I told her I had come to canvass the place; she gave me all the information I desired.

Taking my bundle, I started out; called at the several places of business, and had tolerable good success. I called on *one* gentleman I pitied very much; he had to use crutches. He told me he was a cripple, from rheumatism. Still he seemed energetic, and full of business, carrying on a drug-store and keeping the Post-office, and was contented and happy. He said, when I came around again, he would take Mark Twain's "Innocents Abroad," if I would bring it to him, as he was a great reader. I called at the blacksmith shop, above his place. There was a man working there, an apprentice, I think, who was so low as to be abusive and vulgar, forgetting he ever had a mother.

He was a stout, raw-boned, thick-lipped, flat-nosed, tangle-haired, uncivilized creature, who depended mainly on his strength more than his brains to make his way through the world, and would just as lief strike a *woman* as a *man*. With the exception of this ruffian, I was treated with the greatest of respect by all of the citizens of Mayfield; and was more liberally patronized than I had expected from so small a place.

I returned to the hotel well satisfied with my afternoon's work. Next morning I took the first train for San Francisco. When I arrived there, I went directly to my home on Fourth street, where I remained for a week resting myself, as I was very tired and worn out. It was now late in the fall, and I was afraid the rainy season would set in, for I had to canvass Stockton, so I concluded to go at once. I called at Mr. Bancroft's and told Mr. S— my intentions. He offered no objections, and showed me some new engravings they had; most of them were small and cheap; two of them were very pretty, entitled the "Sale of the Pet Lamb," and the "Burial of the Pet Bird."

I was not long in making a selection of those I thought would be most likely to sell; I told Mr. S— he could do them up and send them to me by express. I went to the wharf and took the boat for Stockton. I had a severe headache, and laid down, so I did not see any of the country through which we passed By the time we arrived there I felt much better. I took a "bus" and told the driver to take me to the best hotel in town. I was soon in front of the St. Charles, and was shown into the ladies' parlor, a large, well-furnished room, with a bright fire in the grate. After warming myself for a few moments, I went to my room, which was very pleasant.

CHAPTER IX.

Stockton.

The next morning was Tuesday; I went to the Express Office, where I found the engravings awaiting me. My first visit was to the printing offices, where I received a promise from the editors that they would give me a good notice.

I then commenced to canvass the town; calling at every business house and office, up stairs and down. In this way I worked for two days.

At this time I had finished the business part of the town. Friday and Saturday I canvassed among the ladies, and was well treated.

I must say, that I found in Stockton as many kind and benevolent people as I have met anywhere. For all that, I was so homesick, I could not see a single spot in all the place that looked *nice*, much less *beautiful*.

The editors, true to their promise, gave me an excellent notice in their papers, and continued it for several days, which was of great service to me; and I here return my heartfelt thanks to them for their kindness.

Sunday morning, when I went into the ladies' parlor, I found collected there quite a number of ladies and gentlemen. From their manner and appearances they deserved that title in full.

I soon learned from their conversation that they were from Alabama. A number of gentlemen from the same neighborhood had come to California a year previous, and settled about a hundred miles from

Stockton, where each had taken up a ranch and fixed houses and conveniences for their families. The latter had just arrived the evening previous, and they had come down with their teams to meet them, and convey them to their new homes.

It seemed hard to hear them talking of their old homes, back in the Southern States; how well improved and convenient they were; their husbands telling how rough and uncomfortable their new ones would be. There was one of the gentlemen they called Doctor, a tall, fine looking man, past the middle age, his hair quite gray. It seemed hard to see a man at *his* age have to give up a good home, and make a new beginning.

His wife was a neat, stylish looking lady, much younger than himself, and I should judge was his second wife, from the different appearances of the children; some of them were very large and others small. In describing their new house to her, he said it was a low, rough, one story building, without even a loft. She replied, "How does that come? At home there was a loft over the carriage-house." He answered, "I wish our new dwelling was *half* so comfortable as that same carriage-house."

Just then a negro girl, somewhere near eighteen years old, entered the room, carrying a sickly looking child, of about two years. She gave it to the Doctor's wife, saying, "Dis yer chile cries all de blessed time."

They told the girl not to go away, as they wished to attend church, and wanted her to stay with the children. I saw no more of them, except when they came down to the dining-room to their meals.

Monday morning all the wagons were in front of the door, many trunks and satchels were stored away; also, provisions and some farming utensils. There were rough seats prepared for the ladies. In a very short time everything was ready, and they began to move away. Many of the ladies said it was a new way of traveling, but they seemed happy and contented. I looked after them, and silently wished them much happiness and prosperity in their new homes.

I now hurried into the street, determined to finish my work, and return home on the afternoon boat. In this I was very successful, as four o'clock, P. M., found me on board, bound for San Francisco.

From the deck of the steamer I had a good view of the surrounding country, and was not very favorably impressed, as it seemed too low and marshy.

The river is very crooked. Sometimes I could see a small sail-boat, which looked to be in an entirely different direction from the one in which we were going, when, all of a sudden, the first thing I would know the steamer was right alongside of it. The river was very low, and it was sometimes difficult for the boat to turn in the short bends. At a few places the steamer stopped, but the towns were small. Nine o'clock, Tuesday morning, found me at home, figuring up how much I had made while I was away. And, to my great astonishment, I found I had made over one hundred dollars.

For the next two weeks I worked in the city nothing of importance occurring during that period After that I concluded to take a run down to San José and finish up my work there; from that place I went to Santa Clara; also, went out in the country to Mrs W., and took her the Lincoln and Washington families pictures she had previously ordered; there I remained until after lunch, when I returned to Santa Clara, and went to the hotel.

The landlord tried to joke me about the earthquake, telling me I had better not go inside, for fear of another. In reply I told him I thought his hair curled much tighter than it did before the last shock. That afternoon I returned to San Francisco. This being Friday, I remained at home until Monday morning.

Half past four o'clock that afternoon found me on board the boat, bound for Stockton again.

The bay was very rough, and the wind was so cold I could not stay long on deck; but, from the window in the cabin below, I had quite a good view of the surrounding hills as we passed; they looked nice and green, as there had been a few slight showers.

When I arrived in Stockton, I took a "bus" for the Eagle Hotel, as I had been told it was much cheaper than the St. Charles, and the fare was just as good; when we reached the Hotel, I must acknowledge it did not look very inviting from the outside. I was shown to a room at once; as I passed the ladies' parlor, and up the stairs, everything looked neat and tidy; once inside of my room, I found it very comfortable.

Next morning I called at the City Attorney's office. He treated me kindly; during our conversation I learned he was a Mason and an Odd Fellow, and had taken the Rebecca degree.

Taking my order-book for a guide, I called on all who had subscribed, filling my orders, and in some places, selling some small engravings in a liquor store. The proprietor insisted upon my drinking some wine; I thanked him, but declined.

We had quite an argument on temperance, but I cannot tell which came out better. I started for the Flouring Mill. On the way, I noticed a policeman

MY ARREST AT STOCKTON, CAL.

following me, but did not care, as I knew I had not been guilty of any crime.

At the Mill I offered the engraving for sale; when I came out the policeman stepped up to me, and said, "Madam, have you a license?" I told him no, that I did not require any. He replied, "You will have to come along with me, and we will see about that. If you don't come along peaceably, I will have to arrest you."

I acknowledge I was angry, and somewhat frightened. I was then forty-three years old, and had never been in a lawsuit of any kind, and always had a great horror of them. I told him I would go with him to the City Attorney's office, for I *knew* he would see justice done me.

The policeman did not have much notion of going there. As I walked up the street, with him close beside me, also the usual battalion of urchins that are always ready to gather around when there is a disturbance of the peace, I was so hurt and mortified, that, by the time I reached the Attorney's Office, it was awhile before I could tell him of my situation, for weeping. He tried to cheer me with his kind words, saying he thought I did not require a license, but he would go and see the County Clerk. The policeman seemed bewildered, and could not understand why the attorney should take such an interest in me. This was the second time the Rebecca degree had been beneficial.

Bidding me remain in his office, he went out, but soon returned, saying it was all right, I did not require a license; also, said the policeman ought to be made to pay me for the time I had lost. I thanked him for his kindness, and went to the Hotel, for my mind was in no condition to battle with the rough trials of canvassing.

In the morning I started for the Insane Asylum. It being pleasant, I concluded to walk. In the portion of the town through which I passed, I noticed some fine private residences and grounds. When I reached the Asylum, I was shown into the Doctor's office. He treated me kindly and gave me his patronage; also, permission to go through the Ladies' Department, and over the grounds. He sent one of the gentlemen attendants with me, telling him to introduce me to the Supervisoress, and she would show me through the building. Thanking him, we started out, and first went over the grounds belonging to the gentlemen's department. They were nicely laid out, with broad gravel walks, well shaded with natural and ornamental trees, bordered with flowers and shrubs. The columns of the porches were covered with creeping vines and ivy. On our way to the Ladies' Department, I saw quite a garden of small fruit and vegetables, which did great credit to the cultivators. In front of the building there were also many very beautiful flower plots.

In the hall, the gentleman requested one of the lady attendants to show me around, as the Supervisoress could not be found. We passsed up the stairs into a large hall, on either side of which were a row of rooms, containing each a bed and other necessary furniture. All was scrupulously clean. There were many ladies sitting around; some of them looking very melancholy, with downcast eyes, seeming to be unconscious of anything that was passing; others were laughing and chatting, and looked and acted rationally. One of them came forward; the attendant told me to speak to her, as she liked to be noticed. She was dressed in a gaudy manner, wearing a dress of highly colored silk, with heavy rich lace fastened about her head, and trailing on the floor.

The attendant said she had gone deranged about dress, and imagined she was a great queen. Bidding the imaginary queen good-day, I passed into a room at the end of the hall; inside, the walls and windows were completely covered with pictures, painted on different pieces of paper, from two to eight inches square, in highly colored paints, in fantastical shapes. The lady artist was in bed, and looked very feeble.

The attendant said she had gone insane while taking drawing lessons, and imagined herself a great painter. The attendant offered to take me to some of the rooms where the patients were violent. I thanked her, and said I did not wish to go. I have visited the Asylums in Lexington, Kentucky, and Columbus, Ohio. In each I saw many lady patients, and I must say of all the insane people I ever saw, there were not any of them had a good shaped head. The majority had very low foreheads.

When we reached the hall below, I thanked the attendant and took my leave. As I passed out through the grounds, I could hear the screams of the raving maniacs, in both the ladies' and gentlemen's departments. I then took a solemn vow that I would *never again* visit an Insane Asylum, unless I should be so unfortunate as to have some friend or relative confined there.

CHAPTER IX.

San Francisco.

On Friday I returned to San Francisco. It was now just one week before the Christmas holidays, and as I had worked faithfully for four months, I concluded to take a rest and make some preparations for them. They passed off very pleasantly. In walking around town, I was struck with the brilliant display of toys and eatables, which certainly give good spirits and light hearts to the community at large. I must candidly admit, that in all the large cities I have been, I never saw so much good taste and cleanliness displayed in decorations as I have in San Francisco.

On February the first, I commenced canvassing again, adding to my stock of engravings, "Washington Irving entertaining his literary friends at Sunnyside;" also three others, entitled, "Life's Day," "Morning," "Noon," and "Night." The three latter were very handsome for to be so cheap, and they made a fine group.

I concluded to try among the private families. I called at many houses on Stockton, Powell and Sutter streets. At some of them it was impossible to see the lady of the house; the impertinent servant girls would almost always shut the door in my face. At several places, where I would succeed in getting into the hall, the women would come to the head of the stairs, and in a very unladylike manner, holler, "What is it you want?" After politely introducing myself and business, scarcely waiting until I had finished, they would say, "No, I don't want anything. *Biddy, show that woman* out." Of course, I had no alternative but to leave.

Working this way very faithfully for four weeks and getting but *little* patronage, and not even meeting with but very few that I would call *ladies*, I became so disgusted that I made up my mind I would *never* try the private families in this city again. I *dislike* very much to say anything against my own sex; and when I am misused by them I feel it keenly. I can stand a rebuff from a gentleman much better, and with less pain; for when I go canvassing amongst them, I look at it in a business point of view, and expect to meet many who will speak to me abruptly; but I must say, with but few exceptions, I have always been treated with a very great deal of kindness and respect among the gentlemen.

After having remained at home for a few days, I started once more to try amongst the shipping. Here I met with good success, selling many engravings and taking many orders for "Mark Twain's Innocents Abroad." I had sufficient employment to keep me busy for several months amongst the shipping, wharfingers, and lumber-merchants.

In this way I finished my first twelve months' canvass, nothing *more* of importance occurring than I have already related.

But one thing I must acknowledge, that if any one of my patrons had looked into my rooms the night previous to my starting to canvass, and had seen them one year from date, would say it was the best money they had ever spent for benevolent purposes.

On August 15th, 1869, I concluded to actually turn book agent, in connection with two chromos, entitled, "Masonics' and Odd Fellows' Charts;" the title of the book was the "Mirror of New York," or, "Life and Sensation in and about the City."

On the book, I was allowed south of Market street as my district; the charts I carried with me and sold on the spot, without having the trouble of going over the ground again. As my commission was very small, I was not restricted to any particular part of the city for them, so I traveled over the whole of it. This gave me steady employment for six months, and was the most pleasant canvass I ever made; not meeting with but very few rebuffs. I also had taken a great many orders for the book, and delivered them during that time.

It was *now* the month of March, and Mr. Bancroft wished me to make another trip to San José, with a book entitled, "The Ladies of the White House." On the 4th of March, I commenced my canvass in that place. Here I worked faithfully for two weeks, and was very successful. Nearly every one I met seemed to recognize me, and treated me with a very great deal of respect. There was one old Judge, who looked up when I addressed him, and gruffly asked if I had any family. I told him I had; he said, "You had better be at home, taking care of them, and not strolling about in this kind of a manner," adding an oath now and then, and offering to bet his old hat that I could neither make a loaf of bread, or wash and iron a shirt. I informed him very politely I could do both. He replied, "I would rather *see* it than hear *tell* of it, as I doubt it very much."

There were two or three *other* persons in his office at the time, who laughed very heartily when they considered he was getting the best of me; I, for the first time since I had commenced canvassing, made up my mind not to be beaten. Taking a chair, I seated myself close beside the Judge, saying, "I know you are an old bach, and likely a woman hater; but, still you must listen to me for a short time." I then explained to him the position I was placed in, and showed him the necessity of me having to canvass; I told him I was no strong-minded, woman's rights advocator, as that seemed to be his strong point of argument against me. I also said that a *lady* could *be a lady*, and follow any kind of employment that was not too laborious, and in the event of her having performed any duty as well as could possibly have been done by a man, she certainly ought to be as well remunerated for the same.

After some lengthy discussion, for and against, I *actually* was successful in talking him into buying a book. When he had bought, and paid for it, he complimented me, by saying that there was not another woman in the State could have persuaded him to buy, so I felt proud of my success, and began to think that he was not such a woman-hater after all.

The next morning found me seated in the Western Pacific R. R. cars bound for the so called *city* of Milpitas. When I arrived there, it reminded me of the old saying, that I could not see the town for the houses, which consisted of one hotel, two drinking saloons, one dry goods and grocery store, two blacksmith shops, one harness making shop, and a half a dozen dwellings; but the citizens were *all* very kind and polite. I did not meet a person but who appeared, from their manners and conversation, to be a well bred class of people. Every thing around the hotel was *very* neat and clean.

In this place I took some half a dozen orders, which I considered pretty well, for a small place.

In the afternoon, I went to Washington's Corners. From San José to this place, along the line of the railroad I was delighted to see so many beautifully cultivated orchards, strawberry beds and vegetables, the land seeming to be adapted for that kind of cultivation. I found Washington's Corners about the same size of a place as Milpitas, but the hotel had very few accommodations; still I found the landlord and landlady very pleasant people.

I noticed a large building, the upper part of which was the Odd Fellows' and Masonic hall; I found that most of the citizens belonged to and were proud of the Orders. In this place I was liberally patronized.

The next day I returned to San Francisco; calling at Mr. Bancroft's, Mr. S., the manager of the subscription department, told me he wished I would go to Sacramento with a new book, entitled "The Sights and Sensations of the National Capitol," a book descriptive of Washington City.

The first Wednesday afternoon in April found me aboard the Sacramento boat. When we left the wharf, I was standing on the upper deck; the bay was very calm, and from where I was, I had a good view of San Francisco, Oakland, and the surrounding hills. The scene looked grand to me as it faded from view. About sunset we passed into the mouth of the Sacramento River. The shores looked very beautiful, and I felt sorry when the shades of evening spread their dark mantle o'er the earth, and hid them from my view.

Soon after dark I retired to my state-room, and it was quite late in the morning when I awoke. It did not take me long to complete my toilet, as it was very simple. I went outside and inquired for some one whom I could hire to carry my satchel, and succeeded in getting a colored boy to take it to the corner of Ninth and L streets, as I had a letter of recommendation to a Mrs. W., whom I believed kept a boarding house.

CHAPTER X.

Sacramento.

Upon arriving there, and ascertaining that I could get board, I paid the darkey four bits for his services, being all the money I possessed in the world at that time; I did not feel much alarmed at this, for I had a half dozen copies of the work with me that I felt confident I could soon dispose of after breakfast, and had arranged to pay my board by the week.

After taking possession of my room, which was very neat and comfortable, the lady invited me out to breakfast, where there were several boarders already seated. She introduced me to them, also to her husband, son and daughter.

Partaking of a good breakfast, and having a short but pleasant conversation with many around the table, I returned to my room. Taking two books in my arms, I passed into the street, intending to call upon a few that had been recommended *first*, and as I went, I heard a few outside remark: " There goes another book agent." Being in a strange place, I must acknowledge I did not like the title. I called on four of the parties of my recommendations, and made a sale of my two books. I next visited the editors of the press, and was kindly received by both. In the morning I was pleased to find, in their papers, a notice which tended to make my sojourn in that city both pleasant and beneficial. I now commenced a regular canvass of K street, calling on every person, working hard until night, not even stopping long enough to take lunch. I was very successful, and was treated kindly indeed. Returning to my boarding house, where I spent a very pleasant evening with the landlady and her daughters, I found them both agreeable and intelligent.

The next day I visited the R. R. offices, and on making my appearance before the illustrious and distinguished Govenor S., I was treated with a very great deal of respect, and received permission from him to visit all of the offices, after having himself pattronized me, for which I tendered him my sincere thanks. I then called in every office, and among the numerous clerks; my order book will show evidence of their liberal patronage, for which I thanked them all very kindly. I *here* admit that Rail Road men, as a body, are a class that have treated me very politely, and with but *one* exception, have not been *even* abrupt in their manner; this fellow was in the employ of Mr. J., the superintendent of the road from Sacramento to Folsom. He was a baggage master, by the name of L. He came up to me, and offered to shake hands. Without being impolite, I could not very well refuse, at the *same* time telling him that I did not remember ever meeting him before. With a hateful grin, he said, "you cannot play that on me; didn't I see you in San José, the week before last, working on this same book?" reaching his hand for the prospectus, which I refused to give him, saying, "you are very much mistaken, I *was* in that place, but had a *different* book."

"I presume you take me for Mrs. B.," who was working there on the same book. He answered, "you need not try to play such a game on me, as I know you are that Mrs. B.; probably if you don't want to recognize *me*, you *would* recognize Mr. F., the engineer, if he would come around. Probably, you will *also* deny making a row between him and his wife, a few weeks ago."

Finding it was impossible for me to convince him of his mistake, and seeing that he was a ruffian under the influence of liquor, and as I had tried hard to get away from him and his abuse, he persisted in following. At a little distance, I saw a Mr. J—, (I *think* a son of the Superintendent) who wore an emblem of Odd Fellowship, and was pleased to find that he had taken the Rebekah degree; and immediately inquired of me what assistance I needed. I told him my name and situation as best I could, for weeping. I pointed out to him the ruffian, who stood at some little distance. As he kind of left on seeing me approach Mr. J—, Mr. J— called to him, and told him he must necessarily be mistaken, as Mrs. J. W. L. must be a lady, or otherwise she would not be in possession of certain signs and pass-words. He also told him that if he did not at once beg the lady's pardon he would discharge him from his employ.

The ruffian then came forward, and asked to be excused. I told him it was freely granted, telling him at the same time I hoped, after this, he would treat every woman with respect, until he *knew* she deserved to be treated otherwise. I watched him sharply while we were talking; he did not seem to care for the insulting language he had used, but stood, with a half drunken idiotic grin on his countenance. I pitied him, for he looked as though he had not been raised at all, but was something like Topsy, *growel* up, *along* with a lot of other ruffians.

Thanking Mr. J— for his interest in my behalf, I bid him good-day, and started for the railroad shops. In passing through the buildings, I insisted upon every gentleman I met to buy; was treated kindly, but received little patronage.

As I returned to my boarding house, I stepped into the Chief of Police's Office. Here I was treated somewhat abruptly by some loafers, who seemed to be just hanging around. The Chie fof Police subscribed for the book, and joked me some about having to pay license. I next visited the Water Company's Office, which was in the same building. There were several gentlemen in the office, from whom I received liberal patronage.

I then continued on my way to the boarding-house, tired in both body and mind. When once in my room, and reflecting over the occurrences of the day, I could not help weeping. I thought it was a great undertaking to be a book agent. I worked faithfully in Sacramento for three weeks, and was very successful. I also liked the place. A great many of the streets were beautifully shaded with large trees. There were many handsome private residences and fine grounds; large and commodious business houses, well filled with merchandise of all descriptions; also several well kept hotels.

The Capitol, then in course of construction, had the appearance of being an elegant structure when completed. There were but few of the rooms occupied, and *they* were yet incomplete. The officers were very kind, and each of them gave me their patronage.

I made up my mind to return to San Francisco by the way of Davisville. The portion of the country through which the cars passed, from Sacramento to that place, was, most of it, low and marshy, many miles of the road being built on trestle work. At Davisville I remained over night. I found it a very small village.

In the morning I concluded to take a run down to Woodland; the journey had to be performed by stage; the country seemed to be well cultivated, and contained some splendid ranches.

I found Woodland a beautiful inland town, of, I should judge, about two or three thousand inhabitants, who seemed to be a well raised and intelligent class of people, full of life and energy; every branch of business was well represented. Here I remained two days, meeting with great success among the ladies, *for a wonder*.

I returned to Davisville, and finished my work; there I took the afternoon train for home. I passed through some fine looking country, also two small villages, which I was told were Fairfield and Suisun.

As we went through Vallejo, but a small portion of the place could be seen. The railroad was some little distance from the central portion, and hills rising between it and the town, hid it from view. The day after my arrival home I went to the store, where Mr. S. seemed very much pleased at my success while I was away, and wished me to go immediately to Santa Cruz, with the same work I had in San José, "The Ladies of the White House." I promised to go in a few days.

The second Monday in May at half past twelve found me seated in the Santa Cruz stage, moving slowly away from Santa Clara. We passed some small fruit ranches; further on large fields of grain, which looked as though they would yield abundantly; we crossed a small creek, which reminded me of the streams in the Southern States, so clear and pellucid that every pebble could be plainly seen in its gravelly bed. After crossing this stream, the soil in appearance seemed to change to a reddish cast, and was not near so fertile ; and some places were covered with oak timber.

Shortly after noon, we passed through a small place called Los Gatos, at the foot of the mountains ; here the stage stopped, while the mails were changed ; we started up again and passed over a rough bridge, after which we commenced to ascend the mountains. Three miles from Los Gatos the stage stopped at Lexington, for the passengers to take dinner. This small place, consisting of a hotel, blacksmith shop, stables where the the stage horses were kept, and a few dwelling houses, was built on a piece of table land on the side of the mountains. This is indeed a beautiful and picturesque spot. The horses were changed, the passengers took their seats, and we were soon whirling upward along the side of the mountain again.

In making the short turns where the road would be very narrow, on one side a deep cañon, on the other the steep mountain, at times I feared the stage would overset into the yawning abyss below ; but the scenery was so grand and I became so absorbed in its beauty that my fears were only for a passing moment.

The deep forests, with their tall redwoods and many varities of smaller trees ; while beneath their branches grew large quantities of ferns and flowers, with their many shades and tints. On nearing the top of the mountains were spots where the large trees were cleared away, and there would be a beautiful thicket, with here and there branches of wild lilacs, white and purple. In some places branches of the wild rose could be seen, with buds and flowers. From the time we commenced ascending the mountain until we reached the foot on the other side, the scenery was one of perfect sublimity. I think it would pay any one for their time and trouble to take a trip to Santa Cruz over the mountains, that they might see the beauties for themselves.

It was past sunset when the stage drove up in front of the Santa Cruz House. Here I stopped. The outside of the building looked old, and somewhat rough, but when I entered, I found it well kept; the rooms neat and comfortable. The table was provided with the best *their* market afforded. I was very much fatigued, and so retired to my room. Through my open window I could hear the sad, low murmurings of the sea, as its waves would break upon the shore, with their ceaseless motion.

The next morning I inquired of the landlady concerning the citizens of Santa Cruz who she thought would be the most likely to patronize me. She recommended me to Mrs. J—, saying she was a strong woman's rights advocator, and believed in helping her own sex; I told her I had not much faith in that sect, at the same time relating to her how I was misused by one of them in San José.

She still insisted upon me calling on Mrs. J—, saying, that I would find *her* a perfect lady, and her name would be of great service to me in obtaining others. After receiving her proper address, a short walk brought me to her residence.

She was a widow lady, and the grounds around her house showed her to be a woman of energy and good taste; as I passed up the wide gravel walk, I had some forebodings that she would not treat me pleasantly; the bell was answered by a more than middle aged lady, neatly dressed, and with a smiling countenance, until her eyes fell upon the books that I carried in my arms.

Oh, horror! what a change came over her; her face was drawn into more than a thousand wrinkles, as she partially shut the door in my face, so that I could only see one eye, as she told me she supposed I was selling books, and that she had just bought one the day before from one of you agents, and could not afford to spend money every day for books, all the time closing the door a little, while she was speaking, until it was finally closed in my face. She acted very much as if she was afraid of me. I left with the opinion she was *not* a lady, or at least did not act like one; and my fullest anticipations were realized, as to my being received by the so called woman's rights advocator.

When once more I reached the street, I asked a small boy if I could get to the town by taking the street to the left; he replied in the affirmative. After walking a few blocks, I found myself on the top of a hill that overlooked the town; I must say it looked rather picturesque and beautiful, lying, as it seemed, in a kind of basin, surrounded by hills ; the dwellings were very much scattered, and a great many of them were even built on the tops of the surrounding hills.

I passed down a long flight of steps, and by taking the first road to the *left*, I was soon in the business part of the town, and commenced canvassing the business men, vowing at the same time I would not try the *ladies* again in that place. I must say I was favorably impressed with the gentlemen of Santa Cruz, all treating me politely, and giving me liberal patronage. I spent a pleasant afternoon on the beach, in company with some ladies from the hotel. We also visited the light-house, standing on a rocky point, jutting out into the sea. From the shore below this point looked very rough and rugged, the rock is high and straight, the breakers dash against it in a wild, tempestuous manner, even in a calm, showing the necessity of a beacon light to warn the approaching vessels of their danger in time of storm.

I returned to the hotel, and the next morning took the stage for San José. On arriving there, I went to see the Superintendent of the San José and Santa Clara R. R., as I understood they wished to make a change in their advertising agent. I found him, and succeeded in making a bargain, I agreeing to pay him fifty dollars a month for the privilege of putting two rows of advertisements in the inside, and as many as I wished outside.

I remained in San José several days, soliciting advertisements, and was successful in obtaining about twenty, who signed an article of agreement to let them remain in one year.

When I returned to San Francisco I called on K. & Company, also on Mr. M——, advertising agents, and learned from them the best plan of conducting the business. They recommended me to somewhere near thirty parties, who were then advertising with them, saying probably I could get their patronage.

I obtained twenty of them, and through *my own* exertions I succeeded in getting ten more. They all agreed to pay me from three to five dollars a month. Messrs. K. and M. gave me a great many advertisements, already printed, saving me that expense. I returned my sincere thanks to *them* for their kindness. Arranging everything satisfactorily, I returned to Santa Clara, where I worked steadily for a week, framing advertisements, and putting in a few at a time in the car when it would stop in that place. In this way I managed until each was properly put up. I hired the drivers to keep them in order. Three parties in San José hired the outside of the cars, furnished their own signs, put them up, and agreed to keep them in order, for the privilege of which they payed me liberally.

When I returned to San Francisco, I commenced working on Mark Twain's "Innocents Abroad," which had just been published. This was a very popular book. The City was divided into three districts, making two agents in the City beside myself. With them I had some trouble, as I did not understand their rules and regulations in the business; but the agents were persons meaning to do right, so we soon made every thing satisfactory. With this book I was very successful, working hard and steadily for three months on my territory in the City, with the exception of a few days the first of each month, when I would stop, collect for the advertisements in the street cars, and go to San Jose one day, to settle with the company.

About this time, some gentlemen persuaded my husband to join them in starting a factory, to manufacture shoes, with Chinese labor. All worked well for a few months, when it failed, leaving us in debt. As to whose fault it was, I am not able to say; but I felt the loss of that few hundred dollars more keenly than I did years ago, when many thousands were lost, for I had worked *very hard* for the few hundreds, trying to save enough to buy us a home. After closing my district in the City, I promised to canvass San Mateo and Santa Clara counties, for the same book. In the town of San Mateo I did not receive much patronage, as there was but little business. But at the private residences, on the outskirts of the town, I sold a great many. The husbands of several of the ladies had already purchased the book in San Francisco.

My next stopping point was Redwood City. Here I put up at Mr. A.'s hotel. During the afternoon I visited the lumber yard. In the office was a gentleman, seeming to be very busy with the books. When I addressed him, I found him polite and agreeable. After conversing a few moments, he gave me an order for the book. In the evening, when I entered the dining-room, I noticed he was seated at the table. After dinner the landlady told me he was an old bach., and boarded there. "You just wait," she said, "I will have some fun with him. I will get some of the boys to help me in making him believe you are a widow lady, and try to get him to take you to the ball, which is to come off this evening." I told her I did not attend parties or balls while I was canvassing She inquired my name, and introduced me to said old bach. when he came out from dinner, and some one went so far as to tell him I *was* a widow; still, we did not, for all that, get up much of a flirtation, nor fall desperately in love with each other, for I think he would not be so easily caught by a stranger, especially a *book agent*. I know I did not wish to get rid of my husband; one man is trouble enough, without having two.

In the morning I called upon Mrs C. Her house and grounds are as fine as any in the place. I found her neatly dressed, and a lady in manners. I knew, from her very countenance, she was a kind-hearted and noble woman. Thanking her for her patronage, I started for Mr. S.'s house; he was at home, and purchased the book I carried. His wife had every appearance of being a perfect lady.

I canvassed all the business men, and found them liberal and courteous, even to the colored "brodder," the barber.

I remained at the hotel over night; ten o'clock next morning found me in San José. While working there, I met on the street one day a widower; he was a Missourian, a fair specimen of southern chivalry, with light hair and blue eyes, which spoke volumes of love as they looked into mine. Using all the persuasive powers he possessed, which were not many, for me to accompany him to his ranch, a few miles from San José, he told me he knew I would make a good stepmother, for I was the mildest and pleasantest *old maid* he had ever met, and would give me a good home, so I would not have to go around the streets, peddling books for a living. While he was making this long, heart-smashing speech, I stood all attention, now and then smiling, which seemed to give him courage, for he was awfully bashful; I could not tell whether he blushed or not, for when I first met him his face was so red from the effects of the tangle-log whisky he had drank.

I told him my husband might object to his proposition. At this he seemed very much surprised, and said, "Why, are you married?" I told him I had been for seventeen years, to which he replied, "darn them fellows, they said you were an old maid, and on the marry." I told him he had better return to his jolly friends, and acknowledge himself sold; probably they would treat him, for after such a long love-making harangue, he must certainly be dry; bidding him good day, I continued my work.

When my business was completed in San José, I had sold sixty copies, which was doing well for that place. I hired a team to take me to Saratoga Springs. The country through which we drove was beautiful. Just this side of McCartersville we passed a grove where they were holding camp-meeting. The driver promised the young miss that was accompanying us that he would stop as he came back; she never had been at a camp meeting, and wished to see the performance.

At the village we stopped, and went through the paper mills. I was surprised to see what a good quality of brown paper was made from straw. When we came outside, Mr K., the proprietor of the mill, introduced me to the ex-senator of Santa Clara County, who looked, from his dress, more like an *exile* than anything else, and from his swaying walk, as he passed to and fro in front of me, lofty manner, when he found I was a book agent. I know he had a very poor opinion of such low, degraded creatures, that go strolling around the country peddling books. I saw he kept his eye on all he possessed, as though he was afraid I might run away with the rocky hills, small bottom land, carrying along with me the grist mill, dry goods store, and rob him of the title of postmaster. We drove away, leaving him still lord of all he surveyed.

As we passed up the cañon, the scenery was beautiful. When we reached Saratoga, Congress Hall was deserted, for it was too late in the season for visitors.

The proprietor of the hall at this time, was Mr. U. His mother was also stopping there, for the benefit of her health, as she was almost gone with consumption. In a few weeks after I was there, she returned to Santa Clara, where she died in a short time.

The Springs were quite a distance from the hall, so we drove over to them. We crossed a beautiful stream of water, and commenced ascending the hill. The road was very good, while on either side was a thick forest. While riding along, a gurgling sound could be heard, as the water passed over its rugged and stony bed.

When we had nearly reached the Springs, we came in sight of a rough building, where men were bottling the water, preparatory to its being shipped throughout the country. The Springs looked as though they received little or no care. The nature of the water is too well known to need any explanation from me. I cannot say I liked the taste of it. As I wandered around this wild and romantic place, although not having such a renowned reputation as the Saratoga in New York, I thought it, in its quiet, natural state, a more suitable place for invalids and persons wishing to get away from the cares of business, and noisy confusion of a large city, than that bustling fashionable resort.

On returning to Santa Clara, we stopped at the camp meeting. It was held in a beautiful grove. As I looked at the minister's rough pulpit, the rows of seats, the tents, wagons and smaller vehicles, it all had the effect of making me homesick. It reminded me how often my dear mother, who has for many years slept in her quiet grave, when I was a child, would take me once a year to camp meeting, for she was a Methodist; not the kind of to-day, who go to church to show their new dresses or fine bonnets, but a plain, old fashioned, true Christian, one who lived up to what she professed, and tried to rear me, her only child and idol, to follow in her footsteps; but I frankly confess, although I have never forgotten her counsel and advice, I am far from being the woman *she* was.

I remember once attending camp meeting in Ohio with my husband. There were a few mischievous fellows, who had been making a great deal of disturbance in the evenings. One of the ministers said he believed he could find out who they were, so he watched them closely, until he caught them at some of their pranks. He was a revivalist, and very popular. He went among them, and putting his arms around their necks, insisted upon their coming up to the altar to be prayed for, at the same time making long chalk marks on their backs, thinking it was too dark in that portion of the ground for them to discover what he had done; but they by some means discovered it, and succeeded in chalking *him*, without *his* knowledge.

The next morning, when services began, this minister arose, and said the roughs that were causing the disturbances would be known by the chalk marks on their backs; at the same time, he turned to sit down; on his back were two or three long white marks; all that saw them roared with laughter, for not another person on the grounds could be found so marked; after that he went by the name of the "Rough Revivalist."

I stopped in Santa Clara for a few days. I had now been in this place at all seasons of the year, and think the climate cannot be excelled anywhere. As Mr. C. keeps a first class hotel through the Summer, he cannot find accommodations for all the persons making applications for board. When I reached the house, I found Col. Albert Evans waiting for me, to take hold of his work in the city, entitled "Our Sister Republic." With this I was very successful, and all treated me pleasantly, for he had many friends. This book gave me employment until the holidays.

CHAPTER XI.

Return to San Francisco.

In February, 1871, I concluded to sell out the advertisements in the street cars, and start a boarding and lodging house. It was the worst move I ever made. I rented a house on Minna street, between Eleventh and Twelfth, suitable for that purpose. I started with six boarders, but in one month's time I knew I could not make anything. I hired a Chinese boy, and tried canvassing and keeping boarders, together. I found it a laborious business; still I kept it up for a year.

During that period, I worked in all parts of the city, on several books; among them, "Knots Untied," a work written by a New York detective; "Garnered Sheaves," by Richardson; "Poetry and Songs," by William Cullen Bryant; "Cuba, with Pen and Pencil;" "Life of Barnum," and "Woman's Pilgrimage in the Holy Land."

While I was canvassing for "Garnered Sheaves," on Stewart street, I called in at one of the piers. As there were a great many ladies canvassing, by this time the men began to be more cheeky. Mr. P— joked me very roughly; so much so, I could not help weeping. He asked my pardon, but I must allow it was not very freely given. On the corner of Folsom and Spear streets I received five orders the same afternoon, which helped to cheer my drooping spirits.

While I was canvassing for the "Life of Barnum," on California street, I went down three or four steps into a large room, where there were quite a number of little offices, divided by railings, each containing a desk and one or two chairs. In the farther end of the room was one quite large office, with four or five men in it. I will not call them gentlemen; they do not deserve that title.

When I first entered, I noticed them whispering, looking toward me, blinking and winking, as though they thought I was very green, and they could play almost any kind of a prank upon me. When I went up to them, one took my order book from my hand very impolitely, looked it all through, saying, " Barnum is an old humbug; still my friends and I will each take a copy, to help you along. We are all friends, and strangers in the city, and will not remain but a few days. Will you bring the books to our rooms, and can you bring them immediately?" I told him the books were ready to be delivered right away. I would comply with his request, providing he would give me the directions. Two of them pretended to sign their names in my order book. One's address was the Cosmopolitan, the other the Occidental Hotel.

I felt confident at once they were fictitious names; but I thanked them all the same, thinking inwardly, you will find I am not so green after all. I stopped at several of the other smaller offices. As I left the room and passed up the steps, one of the pretended gentlemen, who had not signed for the book, was standing outside, and said, "Madam, if you will tell me where you live, I will call at the house and buy a book." I told him I lived in San Francisco. He replied, "Well, I declare, that is satisfactory." "It is all the satisfaction you will get from me, sir," and I passed on.

I went directly to the hotels, and found no such persons stopping there. I was very much annoyed, and studied for some time what course to pursue. I made up my mind to find out their real names, and compel them to take the books, if there was any law to do so. In three hours from that time I knew who they were; as to who gave me the information, it is no fellow's business. I secured four copies of the books, in two styles of binding, and watched the office for several days before I could catch them all in. When I *did*, I marched through the room, with my four books, into their office. I addressed them politely, calling them by their *right* names, saying, "You mentioned no style of binding, so I have brought both; you can take your choice."

They seemed very much confused, made several efforts to say something, but did not succeed. They took the *best* binding, and paid me for them, all the time trying to laugh; said one of them, "You are a Yankee woman, sure enough." I told him he was very much mistaken, for I was a Southerner, and was now even with them. Feeling as though I was victorious, I left the room.

In January, 1872, finding I could not make anything keeping boarders and lodgers, I sold a portion of my furniture, and moved into a smaller house in Hayes Valley. There were two of the boarders I could not get rid of; they said they would be no trouble; so I kept them.

On the first of March I called in Mr. Roman's bookstore, to secure territory for Mark Twain's book, "Roughing It." They gave me Santa Clara county, and a portion of the City. The book was not expected from the East for several days; so I worked on miscellaneous books until its arrival.

One day, when I was in the Subscription Department at Roman's, I was introduced to two ladies, one of them medium size, the other very small. When I learned

A HARDWARE DEALER ON HIS DIGNITY.

they were canvassers, just starting in the business, I pitied them, although they looked smart enough to fight their own battles; for I knew the trials they would have to contend with.

When I commenced on Mark Train's "Roughing It," I found the *small* lady had the district in the City adjoining mine. There was an M. B. we both had to contend with; *his* district was one side of Market, and one of Mission, from the Bay to Sixteenth street. Instead of working on his *own* district, he was like a wandering Jew, all over creation, and caused me to receive a great deal of abuse; when I contended for my rights, I found a great many in *my* district who had patronized *him;* they told me he came into their offices, which were many of them four or five blocks from his territory, to obtain their orders, and they could not very well refuse him, as he was a friend of theirs. It grieved me very much to think he would act so, when he knew my circumstances, and I had taken him for an honest gentleman.

While I was working on this same book, I called in a store where there were two proprietors. As I entered, one was standing in the door-way; when I asked him to buy, he gruffly said, "I don't want any books." I passed him and went inside, which I suppose was very unladylike, and had the impudence to ask one of the clerks to buy; while I was speaking to him, the other proprietor stepped up to me, saying, "What in h—l are you doing here? You had better get out, or I will show you the door; there are getting to be too many of you women strolling around, but it is only an excuse to get amongst the men. *You* are getting most too *old;* you won't stand much show in *picking up a man to live with.*"

I stood my ground, and did not fall on my knees at his majesty's feet, nor ask his pardon for entering his store ; but straightened myself to my fullest height, and took a bird's eye view of him, as he stood with his hands crammed in his pants' pockets, with a thousand frowns upon his countenance, looking as though he would like to devour me ; he was very tall, round shouldered, and light complexioned. As I could not imitate him by putting my hands in my pockets, as I had but one, I deliberately laid my order-book down, and folded my arms, still continuing my view, when he said again, " get out of my store, you trollop." I answered, " You will please to give me a little time, and I will. I wish to see if you are a man, or a brute ; you look something like a man ; you have his form and image, if you wouldn't wrinkle your face so much ; still your actions are *certainly* brutal." I took up my order-book, and started for the door ; when on the steps I turned and told him I already had a husband, and knew how to appreciate him, for he was a *gentleman;* even if I had none, he need not be afraid, for I would not trouble him.

I had much to annoy me, notwithstanding this was the most salable book I had ever worked on. In many of the stores on Front street, I took from three to five orders a day. In canvassing Battery street, I went up stairs in a building occupied by Government employees. In the front room were half a dozen gentlemen, who treated me kindly, but said when I insisted upon their buying a book, " I cannot; my wages are too small, and I do not feel able. I passed into the office. There was a gentleman I will call Mr. W., who had patronized me heretofore. Off from this room was a small private office; the door was open;

AN INTERVIEW WITH A BULLFROG GOVERNMENT OFFICIAL.

seated inside was a gentleman, whom I politely asked to subscribe for Mark Twain's "Roughing It." He said, "I would be pleased to do so, to assist you, but I have already subscribed for a copy." "You will please to excuse me, sir," I replied, "but where did you buy, and who of?" He had not time to reply, when I heard a peculiar noise, something like a big bull-frog croaking. I looked around, wondering how it came in the room. There I beheld, seated in a chair at a desk, a being, something in the form of a man, but in reality looking more like a frog; for he seemed to hold his breath, and swell himself up after the frog fashion, blinked his eye, scowled his face, and croaked out, "What in the h— d— m— is it your business, where he got the book? Any one has as much right in this city as you have. You surely do not think *you* are going to run it. There are a d—m sight of you woman going around. Pretty soon you will be wearing the breeches. You seem to be *one* of them, that think a man has no rights at all. I can tell you d—m plainly where he bought the book; it was in this office, and I bought one too from a Mr. B—, and it is none of your d—d business." I tried to explain to him how the territory was divided; it only seemed to enrage him the more, to think *I* would *dare* to speak in the presence of the majestic frog. He held his breath again, swelling up his jaws, and whirling around in his chair, when I was much surprised to see he wore two emblems. I was already very angry, but the sight of those grieved me to tears, to *think* I was so closely connected to a frog; but then I consoled myself with the idea that it was no blood connection. I know those orders are liable to be deceived and imposed upon by men who join for nothing but selfish motives and popularity. I understood afterwards, his great sympathy for his brother B—, who he said was in reduced circumstances, but who, I heard, was indebted to him in the small amount of thirteen dollars; and *he* promised to get *him* all the subscribers he could, provided he would settle with him. They say this same frog is very benevolent, but I think his benevolence is like a great many others, give very liberally when they think it will be sounded far and wide; but let any person that is poor and worthy come to them for assistance, I am positive the frog, especially, would spurn them from his presence. If, by blinking his eyes, scowling his face, he could tramp them any lower, he certainly would, forgetting *he* was once poor and made his money by washing the filth and dirt from the clothes of the general public, which I think is just as degrading a calling as being a book agent.

For my *own* part, I do not think either degrading, if honorably and properly conducted; but this big bull frog was *now* a government official, and liked to show his authority. It grieved me very much to think that my sons should give their lives in helping to sustain this government, that would hire such a ruffian, who would take the liberty to curse and swear at me in such a manner. I *never* rejoice in any one's downfall, but this frog I believe has had his most auspicious personage dethroned; I expect he has gathered a good deal of *moss* to beautify his hilly but sandy home; there may he rest in peace, and may he *never* have an apportunity to gather any more *moss* from *this* government.

I next visited the Custom House, but found it impossible, under my present excited state of mind, from the abuse I had just received, to solicit any more that day;

so I returned to my home, where I remained for several days. When I commenced work again, I determined to ask no questions, when any one said they had already purchased the book. I was five weeks working my district in the city, and was more successful than I had ever anticipated; I would often think that I myself was most assuredly ROUGHING IT.

CHAPTER XII.

Calistoga.

It being now the anniversary of my marriage, and having always celebrated that memorable day, I concluded, in company with some friends, my husband and daughter to take a trip to Calistoga, and for a few days to try and throw aside the cares and trials of every day life. Four o'clock Saturday afternoon, May 25th, found my friends, family and myself aboard the steamer New World, en route for Vallejo. It being a very pleasant afternoon, we all seemed to enjoy the trip on the bay; arriving at Vallejo at a quarter to six in the evening, and after getting aboard the cars, we had to remain half an hour, for some reason better known to the Railroad Company than to us; at quarter *past* six we left, bound for Calistoga.

The country through which we passed for some miles, I was not favorably impressed with, in its appearance, but as we neared Napa City, we passed some fine ranches; the city is not so large as I anticipated; *that* was my impression from passing through it, on the cars.

From Napa to Calistoga the country seemed to be well cultivated and adapted for the grape. In the upper part of the valley we saw some splendid vineyards. At Yountville there was a large wine cellar; they say it was well filled with wines, and in a flourishing condition.

When we stopped at St. Helena, a great many of our passengers left us, bound for the White Sulphur Springs. We saw many different kinds of conveyances, from the fine carriage with its beautiful horses to the rough farmer's wagon with its rawboned span of mules, that had, as Mark Twain says, "scarcely any tail at all." It was now getting dark, and as we could not amuse ourselves by viewing the country, we then began to realize the grand mistake we had made in not taking dinner aboard the New World; so that by the time we arrived in Calistoga, we were all in a famishing condition. On arriving, we were driven to the Cosmopolitan Hotel. There we engaged rooms; and scarcely waiting to lay aside our hats, wash the dirt from our faces, much less brush the dust from our clothes, we rushed into the dining-room, telling the landlord we were almost starved, and wanted him to send on the table all the Cosmopolitan could afford, as we felt able to devour the whole town, springs and all.

After partaking of a good supper we seated ourselves outside on the porch for a short time, as it was very pleasant. We then returned to our rooms, proposing to meet early next morning in the parlor, and visit the Springs. In the morning, before sunrise, found us all on our way to the Springs, a short distance from the Hotel. When we entered the grounds, to the right was a neat row of cottages, while to the left were several buildings going up.

On both sides of the carriage drive there were a few summer houses, and on the left a small grove, with here and there a narrow path leading to rustic seats beneath the trees.

In the center of the grounds stands the famous Calistoga Hotel, with its porches well shaded with large trees. Just past the hotel is a well beaten path, leading to the famous spring known as the Devil's Kitchen. It was enclosed, forming a kind of room, in the center of which was a small table; upon it were salt and pepper, for the accommodation of visitors desirous of gratifying their curiosity, concerning the length of time taken in boiling an egg—which we performed by placing the egg in a wire bucket, attached to a cord, and lowering it into the spring for five minutes. When we took them out they were boiled hard. After partaking of this romantic breakfast, we visited the several springs. In some places the ground seemed to be very spongy, here and there smoke arising, showing there was a hot spring underneath. On this portion of the ground no vegetation or trees would grow.

The bath houses seemed to be very much neglected. We saw a few parties returning to the hotel, after taking their morning bath.

We left the place, thinking there were more natural wonders than beauties around Calistoga. We returned to the hotel, and after breakfast we hired a team to take us for a morning drive. We took the mountain road to the left. We passed some small vegetable ranches. The driver took us over a very beautiful mountain road, not very steep nor dangerous. The scenery was grand. Some places the trees were so thick and tall that their branches closed and formed a delightful shade. We drove three miles. As we returned, at one point we could obtain a fine view of Calistoga and the surrounding country. When we reached the hotel, the driver told us of another beautiful mountain drive, leading to the famous Petrified Forest; so we engaged the same team for the afternoon. At half past twelve, our party again left the hotel. Taking the road to the right, we crossed a beautiful mountain stream, which we followed for some distance. On either side were the stately mountains, covered with the finest variety of natural trees that I have ever seen in California. We passed two small huts, where the driver told us the wood choppers lived. We now began to ascend the mountain. The road led through a dense forest, and at some places was very steep and dangerous. At one point we passed a team that was driven by a young man at break neck speed. I expected we would both collide, which frightened me very much; but still they passed without doing any damage.

When we reached the top of the mountain we found a small hut where a man kept bachelor's hall, who went by the name of Petrified Charley. He claimed the lands around, and charged every person four bits to admit and guide them through the forest. Each of our party registered his name and address in a large day-book kept for that purpose. In this book were hundreds of names of parties who had visited the forest previous to us, from all portions of the globe. The location of the hut was the most beautiful I ever beheld. There was one of the finest mountain springs, from which our party drank freely of its clear, cold and crystal waters. We found the real owner not at home at the present time, but the place was left in charge of an old shepherd. In company with the old man to guide us, we started for the forest, which was but a short distance, over a small elevation of ground. I could not help but admire how spry and supple the old man of seventy, supported by his staff, seemed to get over the ground, with his long white locks almost covering his neck and shoulders. He was very communicative, and as I listened to his conversation, by his accent I knew he was a southerner; while he told us his son and himself owned a *small* sheep ranch, *as he called it*, of four or five hundred acres, in the mountains, and had upon it several thousand sheep. Also, that they had lived there for many years, keeping bachelors' hall.

As the country looked so wild and uncivilized, one of the party asked him if he was not troubled with wild beasts or bears, when he replied, "Thare hasn't been a bar round these thare parts for many years." I then made inquiry as to which one of the Southern States he was from, and was somewhat surprised to learn he was from my native State, Kentucky. He asked why I thought he was from the south; I answered, " by your accent." We now commenced examining the Petrified Forest, which is certainly a great natural curiosity; to see large trees lying on the ground, turned completely into stone, many of them measuring from three to eight feet across, and *some* had been very tall, showing that they were redwoods, and from their appearance had been petrified while standing, and by some great convulsion of the earth had been thrown down; what seemed more singular, they had all fallen one way, many of them were broken in several pieces, the breaks looking very cragged, the same as a stone will often look when broken. Our party secured many specimens; some of them even showing very plainly the knots on the limbs; many of the trees I examined closely, and found none but what seemed to be solid stone.

In the same forest there were large, thrifty looking redwoods, and the soil around them appeared very rich; but as we wandered farther on it had a white, ashy appearance, with only here and there a sagebrush. At a distance, in a small kind of a basin, was a spot looking as white as though it was covered with lime, but when we drew nearer we found it mixed with a yellow substance, that had somewhat the appearance of brimstone; some of the party broke off a piece. It seemed very hard and solid, as if it had been melted and run together. In a circle of some twelve or fourteen feet in diameter, to stamp on it, would sound as if it was hollow; and when several of the party would stamp on it at once, it made such a terrible noise it would frighten me very much, for fear it would go down. Close to this place were several quite tall points of mountains partially covered with the same white substance, and many of our party joined me in the belief that centuries ago this very spot had been an active volcano. Near this place was a large *partly* petrified tree; from this we obtained some specimens of petrified bark.

The old man also said there was, at a distance of a quarter of a mile from here, a large tree, also *standing*, that was petrified; but as it was getting late and as we did not feel disposed to drive down the mountain road in the dark, we concluded not to go over to inspect it. We now returned to the hut, and I certainly think it would pay any one, for the time and expense, to visit such a freak of nature known as the Petrified Forest.

I regret not being a scientist, and not therefore being able to give a scientific description, as I would like to have done; trusting, however, that the public will receive it in my common-place manner, also the thanks of J. W. L.

Thanking the old man, we left the hut, and began to descend the mountain. We had not gone very far until I became frightened, thinking the driver had lost control of the horses, for they seemed to be traveling like the team we had just passed going up, at breakneck speed; at some places it was so steep it was impossible to keep from sliding from the seat. The younger parties seemed to enjoy the fun, and said I was trying to form myself into a brake, by trying to hold up the buggy. It might have been fun for them but it was none for me, for when I arrived at the hotel my hands were swollen from trying to hold myself in my seat. I may here mention that on our way down the mountain we passed a man on horseback, whom, the driver informed us, was the original petrified Charley, the owner of the land and forest we had just visited. He certainly looked like a rough mountaineer, and I believe was of German descent.

CHAPTER XIII.

Napa Valley.

Next morning some of our party had to leave for San Francisco, to attend to business, but my family and myself remained until Tuesday morning; we took the first train for Napa, where we arrived at half past nine o'clock, and found it a beautiful place, much larger than it appeared when I viewed it from the cars on my up journey. We had heard of a gentleman that owned a fine mountain ranch, some eight or ten miles from Napa City; so we concluded to stop off, hire a team, and make him a call, which I never regretted. After leaving Napa we followed the main road for several miles; then we turned to the right and passed through a large vineyard, and began ascending the mountain. On the side of the road there were some men working; we inquired of them the way to Mr. H—'s ranch, and were told we were now on the direct road to his residence. When we reached the top of the mountain the view was very grand; we could see the Napa Valley, with the beautiful windings of the river. After going along the ridge of the mountain for some distance we commenced descending, and passed through a small thicket of underbrush. In a short time we reached the residence of Mr. H—.

His residence and grounds were situated on a sloping piece of land on the side of the mountain, and I think a more beautiful spot could not have been chosen for a retired private residence. Mr. H. gave us a hearty welcome, showing us around the grounds, and exploring every point he thought would interest us. His house was built in Gothic style, with porches, from which you could get a good view of the three fountains, that were constantly playing, sending up their millions of sprays, to sparkle like so many diamonds when the sun would strike them. They were situated on the sloping ground in front of the house, one just below the other, their waters passing into an artificial lake at their base. In the center of this lake was a small island, on which strawberries and many choice flowers were planted. Around it was a wide path. On the side, shade trees were thickly set. Beneath one of these was a small boat, in which to row to the island or around the lake. On the grounds were many paths around different shaped plots, arranged according to the owner's taste, on which grew a fine and choice selection of plants and shrubs. On each side of the fountains were peculiarly shaped rocks, completely covered with varieties of climbing roses. What made the place seem more beautiful to me, its owner had left groups of natural trees standing here and there, all over the grounds ; underneath were untrimmed, remaining in their wild and uncultivated state.

In some places there were large redwoods sawed down, leaving the trunks just high enough to form a table, around which were seats, on which Mr. H. said his friends held their private picnics. There were several swings and hammocks under the trees close to the lake, and many rustic seats scattered here and there, all over his grounds, while on the porch were lounging chairs. I do not see how any person could live in such a place, surrounded by so many comforts and luxuries, without being perfectly happy. Still, Mr. H. was a bachelor, and said his reasons for so being, were, he was afraid no lady could be contented in so lonely and retired a spot, and he could not give up his mountain home he had taken so much pains to beautify. The fountains and lake were fed from a spring, bursting out of the side of the mountains just above his house. He said this was his reason for settling here, so he could have an abundance of water.

After having shown us all over his beautiful place, he insisted upon our remaining and taking lunch with him; after which he ordered out his team, and accompanied us as far as the foot of the mountain. Stopping on the ridge, he pointed out many ranches and vineyards of note, and showed us how far his lands extended, of which he had several thousand acres. At the foot of the mountain we parted, thanking him for his kindness and hospitality. We arrived at the station in Napa City just five minutes before the starting of the last train that day for San Francisco. We were soon on our way, and reached home about half past eight o'clock in the evening, where we found Polly, the parrot, very much rejoiced to see us.

Here I remained for several days. On the fifteenth day of June I packed up my books and started for San Jose. On arriving, I once more became a book agent, working on Mark Twain's "Roughing It." The citizens of San Jose knew me well by this time, and patronized me liberally. In this place in three weeks I sold one hundred and five copies, which was the largest sale ever made there on one book by any canvasser. With this book I visited Los Gatos. It being such a small place, I was not very successful, and returned to San Jose. The next day I took the stage for the Alameda mines, in Santa Clara County. The road was very dusty and in some places very rough. We passed a number of flourishing looking ranches. When the stage arrived at the town on the flat, I was much surprised to see the store and hotel windows with iron bars across them, something after the fashion of a jail; but I was told it was necessary, on account of so many roughs that work in and about the mines.

The town here consisted of one street; on the lower side of it were many dwellings; at some of them the entrances were lower than the sidewalk; along this side of the street, at the edge of the sidewalk, was a small ditch, through which the water was carried from the mountain stream to supply these dwellings. It was constantly running, being very clear, and, I was told, very cold, although I did not taste it.

At this place is the spring from which we get the Vichey water. I do not know what its medicinal qualities are. I drank freely, and know it was *beneficial* to me the few days I remained there; for I was very near sick on my arrival, and had been for some days, and felt much better from the effects of the water when I left. In the place I did very well, considering the small amount of the citizens that could read English. I returned to San Jose and took the first train for Mayfield; here I sold seven copies. The next day I returned home, where I remained for several weeks.

Mr. Roman wished me to take another trip to Stockton for him, with a work entitled, "The Great Industries of the United States." *This* trip I made by the cars. The scenery around Niles' Station I thought quite beautiful, located as it was in a corner in the mountain. After winding our way through the canon, we arrived in the Livermore Valley; the soil seemed to be very gravelly; but they say it produces fine crops in a rainy season. Livermore seemed a new, flourishing little village. When we arrived at Bantas I concluded to stop. Here I met a gentleman whom I had seen before in San Francisco. He said he would like to buy my book, but did not feel able; but would try and get me some subscribers. He went to the door, looked around, and says, "There is a gentleman, an old bach. I will call him, and tell him you are a widow and want to marry. You must not contradict me. I can then soon persuade him to buy *several* books." He said, "Not long ago our boys played a terrible prank on him. He is very rich, and one of the meanest men we have in the country; so mean that no woman would marry him, not even for his money.

"Our boys knew he was crazy to get married, so they wrote many fictitious letters, purporting to come from some nice young lady in the neighborhood; upon receiving his answers they would answer themselves, saying that if he would send her so much money she would meet him in San Francisco, where they could be married, as her parents were not willing for their union. The old fool took the bait, sent the coin, and at the appointed evening would have gone to San Francisco if some one had not returned him his money and letters. Now if they say anything to him about going to San Francisco, he gets very angry." But my gentleman friend said, "Anyhow, I will call him, and try and get some coin out of him for you." When he came over to where we were standing, he introduced me, saying, "This is Mrs. L—, a widow lady, from San Francisco, selling books." He then told the gentleman to come into the hotel, and he would see how many he could get to subscribe for the book. He afterwards informed me that when he went inside he told I was a hard-working woman, and would make him just such a wife as he wanted, for he *knew* I could make splendid bread, as he *had often eaten at my house;* "and," says he, "if you will show your liberality by buying two of the books she has, I think, without any doubt, you can persuade her to marry, by telling her you have a fine rancho, not far from town, where she could have a good home;" at the same time telling him, "I will sign for a copy myself." They then came out, gave me my order book they had taken in with them, and the old man bought two books, and at once began asking *me* questions that I scarcely knew how to answer.

During the conversation, I mentioned something about my husband. He got very angry, and said I told him I was a widow.

The other gentleman now came up, and repeated the conversation he had with the old man, who seemed so angry that I offered him his money again; but he would not take it, saying I was not to blame, and with a terrible oath, said, "These boys are always playing pranks on me. Now I will get even with them yet, if I blow some of their brains out."

I left them, and reached the depot just in time to catch the train. After I was seated in the cars, I vowed I never would be guilty of allowing any one to falsely introduce me. When the train arrived in Stockton, I took the 'bus for the Eagle Hotel. The next morning I started out as a *book agent*, for the first time in that place, but was not so successful as I had been with the pictures. I worked very faithfully for several days, and scarcely made enough to defray my expenses; returned to my home in San Francisco, where I remained for several weeks.

CHAPTER XIV.

San Francisco.

I next went to work for Mr. Bancroft on a book entitled, "How I found Livingstone," by Stanley; for it I took the central district. While on California street

I went into an office where there were three or four boys, about nineteen years of age, behind the counter. When I entered, they seemed very much tickled at my appearance or business, I scarcely knew which. They huddled together like so many chickens, that their mother had just weaned and set afloat; they tucked down their heads and whispered and giggled, as though they needed some one to teach them good manners. I tried several gentlemen who were in the office, and from one of them obtained an order. He pointed to the giggling boys, and said probably *they* would buy. I told him there was no use showing *them* the book, for I was positive they could not read, or otherwise they would know what good manners were. This book gave me constant employment until the holidays, during which I remained at home, and spent them very pleasantly.

The latter part of the spring of 1873 I commenced working for Mr. Roman on Gen. McClellen's book, "The Golden States, or West of the Rocky Mountains." My district was from the south side of Market street to the bay. While on Stewart street, I stopped into Mr. P's office. He is a lumber merchant. In the office were several gentlemen, among them Mr. K., whose office is a short distance away. Mr. P. said, "you need not come around any more, for *now* we have nice young ladies calling on us every day;" and laughing, said, "you are like myself, getting too old to stand any show; but if you will bring some nice young lady around with you, we would *all* buy a book." Mr K. then said, "I think Mrs. L. would be *afraid* to bring any of her young friends among the rough lumber merchants of Stewart street." I replied, "No, indeed, for I have canvassed this street many times, and the gentlemen, one and all, have treated me with a great deal of respect, with the exception of Mr. P. here." At this they all laughed, saying, "That's a good joke on you, Mr. P." He blushed a little, and joined in their merriment, afterward saying, "That is one for you." I said to him, "Don't you deserve it, for joking me so roughly a year or more ago?" His face became still redder, and he stammered, "I don't remember, for I am always joking with some one." I remembered it very distinctly, and thought we were even now. After trying to get an order for the book, I started to leave the office, telling Mr. P. good naturedly, to be careful what he said to book agents, for they were treacherous beings; bidding them good-day, I tried my luck in the next office.

After canvassing Steuart street I went among the shipping. Here I stood no chance, for the small lady had made such a deep impression on all the sea-faring men that they would not notice so *old* and *homely* a creature as I.

I worked on this book for some weeks. One morning, on the corner of Townsend and Fourth streets, three small boys came out of a saloon; two of them were smoking cigarettes, and one of them a little old clay pipe; I looked at them sharply, thinking how young they were (for they were not *more* than eight or ten years old,) to be on the broad road to ruin. I suppose the one with the pipe thought, by the way I watched them, I was envious of their enjoyment; for he stepped up to me, politely tipped his hat, at the same time holding the pipe toward me, said, "Old woman, won't you have a smoke?" He looked so comical, in spite of myself, I could not help laughing. They all clapped their hands and laughed, like any little hoodlums would. I passed on, and was soon in the blind and sash factory, on the next street; but for some days after I could not help smiling whenever I would think of the boy with the little old clay pipe.

A few days after Mr. Roman wished me to commence work on William H. Seward's book, entitled, "His Voyage around the World." For this I had the central district, being from the south side of California to Market, and from Kearny to the Bay. While continuing this work, I met a young lady I had formerly known in the east. She said during our conversation that she was in reduced circumstances, and asked me what I thought about *her* trying to canvass, and if I would help her in obtaining a situation. She called at my house, and I gave her all the information I could concerning the business, and went with her to secure a chromo, that she could have the privilege of selling on the spot, without taking orders. We started out, I having promised to assist her for several days. As we passed a large business house on the north side of California street, where twenty dollar gold pieces were very plentiful, with many clerks behind a counter to watch them, here I told her we would stop; though *I* never was successful with Mr. R——, I thought she might be, as she was very handsome and young. I led the way, the handsome lady following; and as we passed the counter, towards the private office, even the *quiet* clerks cast admiring glances at her.

We entered the office; just inside the door she took a seat. Mr. R— was at his desk; when I approached nearer, he looked up; when his eyes fell upon me he frowned, and said, "I do not want any book." I did not seem to notice what he said, but called up my friend and introduced her and her chromo; at the same time holding it for his inspection. I do not think he saw the chromo; for when the young lady approached he sprang to his feet, scraped and bowed very politely, saying, "Excuse my abruptness, *ladies*, I was very busy;" all the while never taking his eyes from the lady, which made her blush and look handsomer than ever. I politely asked him to buy the chromo, to assist her. He replied "certainly, certainly;" and handed over the coin.

He took the chromo from her hand and set it to one side, never for a moment faltering in his gaze; as we left the office I turned to close the door. He was still sending his most bewitching glance after her. But I do not *think* he ever had the pleasure of meeting her again, for she did not like either California or canvassing, and returned to her home in the East a short time after.

CHAPTER XV.

Santa Clara.

I was not as successful with Seward's book as I had anticipated, but felt grateful to all those who *did* patronize me. I finished my district in the city in five weeks, and was now ready to be transferred to some other seaport where I might annoy the citizens with another book agent. Santa Clara County, my old stumping ground, was next assigned to me. In San José I had great success; so I concluded to take a run to Gilroy. I was much surprised to see how this place had improved since my first visit, the population having increased to twice its original number. I stopped at the Williams House; found it well kept, under the supervision of Messrs. Fish & Gray. I called in a store where medicines were sold; the clerk was very airy, and asked me a great many questions, some of which I did not feel disposed to answer, when he said, "What in the devil *do* you know?" I told him there was *one* thing I knew, that he thought himself very smart, and *one* thing I would *like* to know: did any one else but himself think so? at which he laughed, very much like an idiot. Some gentlemen came in. I tried to sell *them* the book, when he commenced some of his dirty, low slang. One of the gentlemen reproved him, at which his face became crimson. I said, "Is it possible that you can blush? I thought you entirely destitute of shame. I shall have a better opinion of you in future;" and left the store. I was quite successful in Gilroy. I heard many speak of Hollister as being a lively place, and concluded to try their generosity in patronizing book agents. The country through which the cars passed was very low, but the soil seemed good. When we arrived at the town I stepped from the cars, looked around for a hack or some conveyance to the hotel, which seemed to be some distance away. I saw nothing but a two seated carriage, looking as though it *might* belong to some rancher. I noticed many ruffians of both sexes standing on the platform, and recognized them as being the same party who came aboard the cars at Gilroy. I inquired of the gentleman in the carriage if I could get a conveyance to the hotel. He said "yes, I will drive you there; get in." Just then a gentleman stepped up, who I afterwards learned was clerk in the Montgomery House, saying, "Madam, this is not the carriage; you will find a conveyance on the *other* side of the depot for the Montgomery House."

Away I went, lugging my two baskets; the wind

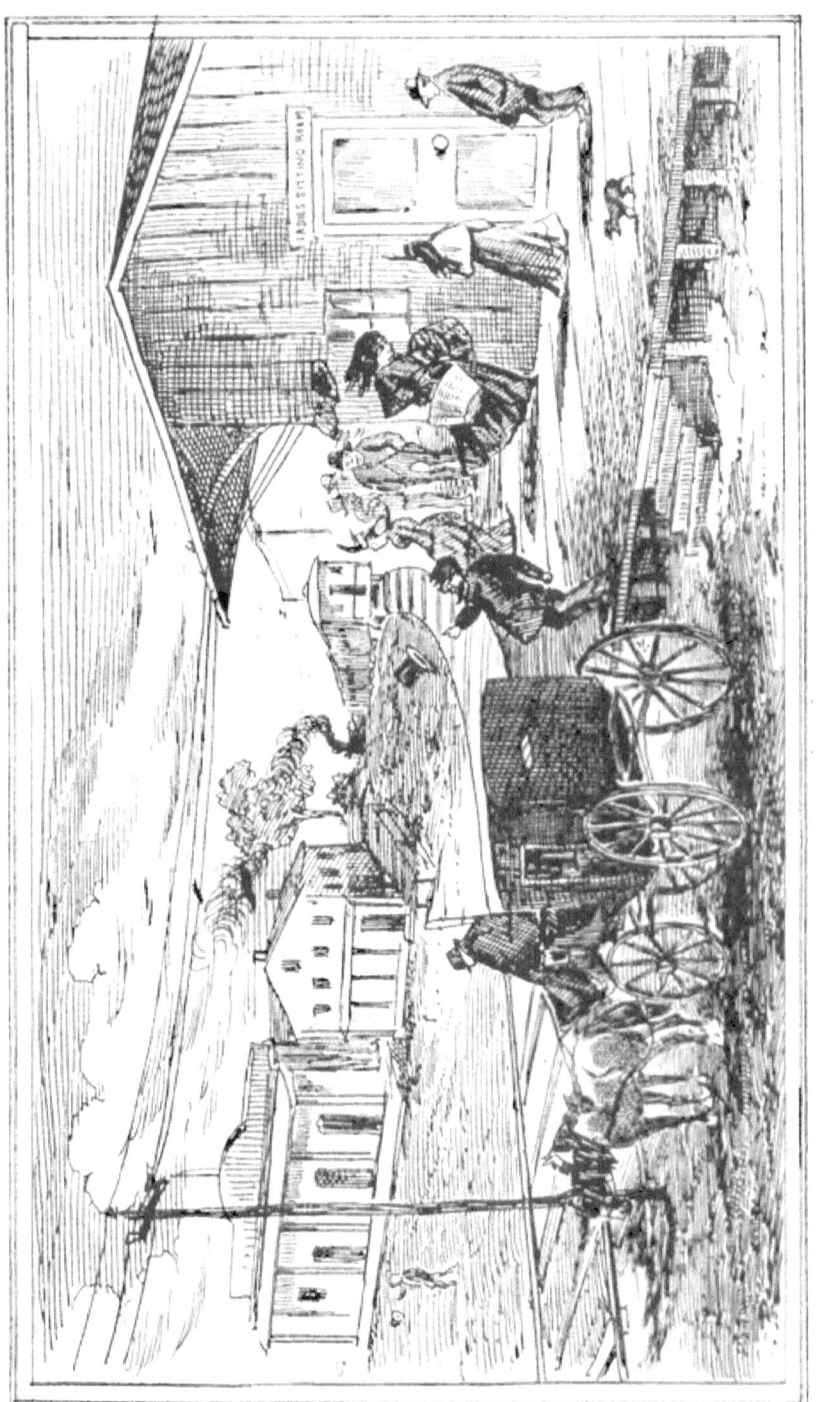

A ROUGH DEAL AT THE HOLLISTER DEPOT.

blew fearfully, and as I turned the corner of the ladies' sitting-room it lifted my hat from my head and sent it whirling up the street. Some kind gentleman picked it up for me, for which I thanked him, and then secured it firmly on my head by tying my veil over it, while the impudent clerks stood laughing at the scene. Upon reaching the opposite side of the depot no vehicle of any kind was to be seen; so I had to retrace my steps, lugging my baskets with me. By this time many of the loafers had gone; while in the above-named carriage was seated a lady from San Jose, with whom I was well acquainted. She called to me, saying, " Mrs. L., here is room for you; come, get in; you don't intend walking to town with all *that* baggage, surely." I asked her if she was going to the hotel, to which she answered, " Yes, to the Montgomery House, the best in the place." " Why, this man (pointing to the clerk) said this carriage was not the *one*." She seemed astonished, and looked first at the clerk, and then at me. He stepped forward, took my baggage, and assisted me to get inside.

I was very angry, and if it had not been so near dark, and I being in a strange place, I would not have accepted the ride, but left my baggage and went on foot. When we reached the hotel I was informed the landlord had received a dispatch from Gilroy stating they had driven a lot of roughs from there, who had taken the cars for Hollister, and to look out for them. This, then, explained the cause of the clerk's singular conduct. I told him it was the first time I had ever been taken for a rough. But I suppose he knew from the way I carried my baskets they must be heavy, and took *me* to be the leader of the gang, who had stolen all the money Gilroy possessed, and had it in them. Being attired in a plain muslin dress, hat and shawl confirmed his belief. When my lady friend in rich attire recognized me, he changed his mind. Probably he, like many others, thinks fine dress makes a *lady* or *gentleman*, but he must not *forget* the old saying, "Never judge from appearances;" for *sometimes*, beneath the coarsest fabric, beats an honest, kind and noble heart. Remember *Our Saviour* was born in a manger, wrapped in swaddling clothes.

Notwithstanding the trouble I had in getting to the hotel, I found it well kept; the landlord and lady were Southern people, very kind and obliging; even the clerk, which I forgave for his treatment, as I *know* he only did his duty. The next day I canvassed the town, found it quite a large place, considering such a few years' growth, very lively, and all branches of business well represented. The citizens were kind and benevolent. The country around the town, as far as I could see, looked in a flourishing condition. Here I sold a number of William H. Seward's books; the first man that bought one of me was the *dead beat*, as I called him, who, you will remember, I had met some years previous, on my first trip to Gilroy; and by the way lives on the same ranche where the monstrous sweet potato and beet were raised. I recognized him at once; when I repeated our conversation in the stage, he laughingly said, "Yes, I remember it well; and the soil is just as productive as I said. If you don't believe me, come and see for yourself." Thanking him for his invitation, I bade him good afternoon.

Next day I went to Gilroy, and from that place directly home. In a few days I entered Mr. Roman's store. He wished me to take Vallejo for William H. Seward's book, which I did. On leaving the boat at South Vallejo I took the cars as far as the junction. There I took a hack for the hotel. As we drove down the street I thought it would be a very difficult place to canvass, being hilly, and the residences very scattering. After reaching the hotel I remained there over night. Next day I crossed over in the ferry-boat to Mare Island. Here the Government has some splendid machinery, which I take as much delight in examining as any great connoisseur; each department seemed to be well conducted: I found the Superintendents kind and obliging. I visited the officers' quarters; there I received liberal patronage. Beyond these the Government has erected a row of neat brick dwellings, surrounded by beautiful grounds. Here the officers make their homes. I called upon their wives; found them also kind; all begged to be excused from buying, saying that they were changed around so much, they did not wish to be encumbered with books. I think Mare Island a beautiful place. In the afternoon I returned to Vallejo. There I worked hard for some days, with but little patronage. I found the citizens all civil and well bred. In this place I spent a very pleasant evening, at the Rebecca Lodge; I must say the pleasantest I have ever spent away from home, in California. They have a nice hall, and the ladies were very sociable. The next day I went to Fairfield and Suisun. I took a rickety old carriage, driven by a darkey; it was quite a distance to the hotel from the depot, and I was afraid the old vehicle would break to pieces before it got there; but it landed me safely at the door. The proprietor I found to be a gentleman who the year previous had a store on Fourth street, San Francisco. As I had called at his store several times to sell him a book, we were slightly acquainted. He introduced me to his wife; the evening passed pleasantly.

Next morning in looking around the town I did not like its location, and the wind seemed to blow a perfect hurricane. The inhabitants did not appear to mind it, but all were bright and alive when it came to business. I never saw or heard tell of so many pianos and musical instruments in a town as there were in that small place.

There was a street they called Piano street, for a nickname. Here I met an old widower, who owned many of the swamps around the town; *good land,* as *he* called them. He said he had a son that was marriageable, and would soon be off his hands; then he would be all alone, for his wife had been dead these many years; all the time looking up into my face, and sending his bewitching glances in that direction. He was seated on an *apple-box* in a *warehouse.* Wasn't that romantic? Continuing his nonsense, he said, "I suppose you are a widow or an old maid, else you wouldn't be tramping about the country selling books." He talked so fast, I did not get a chance to put a word in edgeways. And my friendly readers know, if he could beat *me,* he must have been an extraordinary fast talker. But he finally stopped to take breath, when I told him I was a married lady; also, if I could not sell him a book, I must be going.

On my way to the hotel, I thought what splendid offers I had, if I was only a widow or an old maid; the old widower I had left was something like the one in San José, about half drunk. In Suisun I was very successful; also in Fairfield. Next morning I returned to San Francisco. At home I found awaiting me a letter from Mr. Bancroft, stating he wished me to go to Watsonville and Santa Cruz, with Col. Albert Evans' book, entitled "A la California." I called to see him, and promised to go the next week.

CHAPTER XVI.

Pajaro Valley.

Tuesday following, found me on the cars moving away from Gilroy. In the country through which the cars passed the soil seemed to be well adapted for the tobacco culture.

When we came to Pajaro Valley, I was surprised to see such fine ranches, well fenced; many of them having nice dwellings and barns.

It reminded me *more* of farm life, in the Eastern States, than any place I had seen in California. The soil seemed adapted for all kinds of crops, and many of the ranches had fine fields of corn. When the cars arrived at Watsonville, I took a carriage for the hotel, which I found a fine building; the rooms large, airy, and well furnished. I think Mr. Billings and his wife are *perfect* in the art of managing a hotel; for everything moved along like clock work. I remained at the hotel until next day, resting myself, when I started as book agent in a strange place. Watsonville is a very pleasant little town, the population seeming to be a very intelligent, industrious class, and inclined to treat strangers with respect; but I sold very few books, as one and all, when urged to buy, would say, " there are several agents living here, in our town, who are very needy, and if I buy of any one, I must patronize them." For this I was well pleased with the citizens. Thursday I took the stage for Santa Cruz. In some places the scenery was grand, but nothing to compare with that on the other road, across the mountains; still it was a very pleasant drive. As we neared

Santa Cruz a splendid view could be had of the surrounding country. I stopped at the Franklin House, which was kept by a widow lady, and found both her and her daughter obliging and agreeable; the latter very handsome and stylish. After partaking of a light supper, I retired to my room, as I felt very much fatigued.

In the morning I thought, on this, my second visit to Santa Cruz, I would not call on the benevolent lady, Mrs. J. Taking my basket, I passed into the street, where I made a hasty march toward the Court House, thinking, as nearly all book agents do, I must try the County Officers first. I found them all *perfect* gentlemen, and received two orders; several promised to buy when the books came. I worked all day, with but little success. Next morning, at the breakfast table, I met a young lawyer that I had seen the day previous in the Judge's office. Upon his inquiry as to how I was succeeding, I informed him "not very well." The conversation turned upon the war; when I related to him my losses and trials during the rebellion, and that I lived in Ohio at the time. He seemed to sympathize with me; for he, also, then resided in one of the Eastern States, and took an active part in helping his country. He used his influence outside, and was the means of my selling many copies, for which I was very grateful; and hope he may always prosper, no matter where his lot may be cast. As I have understood, he has since married; I hope his wife may prove a true and noble woman.

The Sabbath I spent in Santa Cruz was very lonely, for on that day I always prefer to be with my family. Monday I worked very hard, and Tuesday until time to take the stage for Soquel. The gentleman who owned the stage resided there; as we neared the town he inquired which hotel I wished to stop at; I told him the best in the place. He replied there was no preference; they were all about the same. No matter which one you stop at; the others will work against you; for they are at swords' points. I told him I would just as lief stop at a private boarding house, if there was one in the place. He said he sometimes kept boarders, and perhaps could accommodate me. I thankfully accepted his offer; so he drove to his residence. When we reached it I found it quite a large and nice looking house. After introducing me to his wife, he went to put away his team, when his wife informed me *she did not keep boarders;* she was very cool, and my presence seemed to annoy her; so I quickly betook myself to Mr. Mann's Hotel, where I procured a room, and in company with a small boy returned for my baggage.

I asked the wife how much my bill was, as I had taken lunch there; she appeared very much astonished to think I was going to the hotel; I told her she had a large family, and I did not wish to annoy her; thought I should feel more at home in the hotel. Returning, I found Mrs. Mann to be as pleasant a lady as I have ever met. I canvassed this large city in three hours, was treated kindly, received but one order, and that from the landlord.

In the morning I took the stage *again,* bound for Watsonville. After stopping at the hotel for lunch, I took the 'bus for the railroad, and came directly to my home in San Francisco. There I stayed until I commenced work on Mark Twain's last book, "The Golden Age," for which I had my old district north of

California street. I worked faithfully on this for three weeks. Nothing of importance occurred during that time; each day seemed to be a great trial to me, for my strength was fast giving away. Mr. Roman was to have the books the fifteenth of December; luckily for me, they did not come until almost three months from that time. During the holidays it was with great effort I sat up. The second day in January I was attacked with a congestive chill, and was not able to leave my room for eight weeks, where I was confined with typhoid fever. When I did commence work again, which was about the middle of March, I was so weak I was afraid to venture out alone.

During my sickness the books had come; as I was in need of the money, and Mr. Roman was anxious to have them delivered, I had to take my daughter to assist me, which I regretted very much. But in a few days I was able to go alone. After filling my orders, I commenced to canvass the balance of my territory that I had not been able to finish before. I found it already thoroughly canvassed by several agents, who *knew I was sick*. Upon my asking them about it, they all denied it. It is an old adage, "Ill got gains never prosper." Whoever they were, I wish them no harm. With "The Golden Age" I was not so successful as with his former two books. As I had not fully regained my strength, I remained at home for a short time, when I again commenced work for Roman, on Josh Billings's book, "Everybody's Friend."

For this book I chose the south side of Market street. I also took San Jose, where I was very successful. Tired and disgusted, I almost made up my mind to retire from the business. I remained at home for some time; but getting scarce of pocket money, and Mr. Roman wishing me to go to Redwood City, San Jose, Gilroy, Santa Cruz, Watsonville, Salinas City, with the Life of Sumner, and Johnson's work, I left the store, promising to start next morning.

CHAPTER XVII.
Santa Clara Valley.

July 14th. Upon waking, in the morning, my first thoughts were, must I again leave my home to go and contend with the rough realities of a canvasser's life? With a heart filled with sad forebodings, and I fear a sad countenance, I prepared for my journey; books packed, hasty breakfast, sad goodbye to dear ones, I started, satchel in one hand and basket in the other, for the Market street cars, which are three long blocks from my residence; at the depot I buy my ticket for Redwood City, which left me only a dollar and a half. Taking my seat in the cars, I amused myself by watching the different faces as they came in. Four ladies attracted my attention by their merry laughter. A few minutes after their husbands came in, with their tickets and checks, followed by four small boys. I soon learned from their conversation that the ladies were bound for Pescadaro, on a pleasure trip. The gentlemen seemed very jolly; one of them inquired what about the boys? the other answered, "Tell the conductor when he comes around there is one apiece." The bell rings, the gentlemen bid goodbye, and leave the car; the signal given, we are off. As the car passed the gentlemen, I thought how happy they looked, because they could send their wives and children away for pleasure and recreation. Wives and children looked happy, also, and I know they were; for their countenances and actions did not deceive. There are many hundreds more who are happy, while others are very miserable.

It is not money or position that makes happiness, but a contented mind, that can withstand the cares and storms of this life. I often look at a grand and beautiful tree, one of nature's own planting, and compare it to the human mind. The rough winds will bend its branches until it would seem as though they would break and fall to the ground; still a light breeze will send them up, and there they stand as straight and majestic as ever. Oh, for a mind and strength of will for one and all to stand the cold rough winds through life, is my prayer. But I have wandered from my subject. There was nothing of importance occurred until we arrived at Redwood City, and I once more became a book agent. I called on Mrs. Dr—, found her not in, and started for Mr. H—'s residence. I passed Mr. B—'s saloon; two gentlemen were seated outside. They both seemed very pleasant, and one signed for a book. The other buys one of Mark Twain's books and pays me the coin. I then continued my way to Mrs. H—'s residence. The bell was answered by the lady in person; I found her, as heretofore, very kind and agreeable; she bought one of Josh Billings' books, and signed for Sumner's. Thanking her very kindly for her patronage, I bade her good morning, and next visited the Court House, where I sold one book and got a few orders. From there I commenced my regular canvass, from one place of business to another. They all seemed glad to see me.

I took about fifteen orders. Just as I was leaving the last place, some one pulled my shawl. On looking around I found it to be a man (he did not act like a gentleman) from San Jose. I told him kindly to keep his hands to himself. "I know you have been very kind in giving me your advertisements, when you were in the insurance business; still, I do not like so much familiarity;" at which he very abruptly said, "What are you following me around for? the next thing I know, my wife will be getting jealous of you." I bit my lips with anger, and informed him his wife, with no disrespect to her, would have to marry a gentleman before she need to be jealous of me. He replied, "I believe you are angry," and left me.

I went to the hotel next. There I remained until time to take the train for San Jose, which was the first train the next morning, July 15th. Taking said train, I left Redwood City. Nothing occurring, I arrived in San Jose in due time. Taking the New York Exchange coach, I was driven to the hotel. Was shown to a room, in which I remained until lunch time. After lunch, I went to Mr. B——'s office on Santa Clara street, and got him to attend to some business for me. I then took the street cars for Mrs. B——s, where I spent the rest of the afternoon and evening. July 16, I returned to San Jose and canvassed all day, and only received four orders; returned to the hotel, tired and disgusted with life.

July 17th. Arising, I make a hasty toilet, and descend to the breakfast table. There were three ladies already seated at the table where I was. They seemed to be strangers in the place; one, an elderly lady, and her daughters. I did not learn their names, or anything about them; but I never saw, in all my travels, sorrow depicted on countenances so plainly as in theirs. I pitied them from the bottom of my heart. Leaving them at the table, I returned to my room and prepared, for the street. Passing down the street, I met Mr.

G——, and asked him to subscribe for a book. He replied, "I am sorry, but I cannot, as I have been almost laid up with my leg." I then observed he was walking with a cane. I inquired what was the matter. He said, "Did you not hear of my mishap? The other day, when we had local option here, Sallie Hart threw me down, run over me, and broke my leg." Mr. G—— and I are the best of friends; so I knew he was only jesting. I next called on Mr. P——, and asked him to subscribe for the "Life of Charles Sumner," for the library. His answer was, "We are not buying any books at present." Mr. J——'s office being in the same building, I visited him, and he subscribed for Johnson's book. He requested me to be seated and rest myself, which I did, and we had a short, pleasant conversation on different subjects. Promising to bring his book the next day, I bade him good afternoon.

In the hall I met Mr. B—, and tried to sell him a book, but without success. The balance of the day I canvassed among the ladies; but without very good success. I do not know why, but with the ladies I can never be successful. Very tired and worn out, I turned my steps toward the hotel. Passing the post-office, I stepped in and found two letters waiting for me. One was from home; the other from Roman's, with a bill for books sent to me by express. As soon as I got to my room, sat down to read my letter from home. It contained no bad news, but still it had the effect of making me very homesick. I thought how different my life was from many others; how glad I would be if I could remain at home with my family, instead of roaming around the country; still I feel it is best for the present. I am anxious to get a home, so we all can be independent. With these thoughts, I retire for the night.

July 18th. This day passed as many others, working hard, and with but little success. This being Saturday, I took the street cars for Mrs. B——, where I remained until Monday morning, enjoying myself hugely.

July 20th. After breakfast I packed my books and left them at Mrs. B——, telling her I would have the stage call for them on our way to Los Gatos. At her house I took the street cars for San Jose. I delivered several books and received pay for them. Returning to the hotel, I settled my bill, and there I remained until the stage bound for Santa Cruz called for passengers. Taking a seat inside with many others, the driver takes his seat and we are off. On our way through the Alameda we stop at Mrs. B—— for my baggage and books.

We stopped at Santa Clara depot to receive passengers from the cars. By this time the stage is pretty well filled. Again we are off. The drive from Santa Clara was very dusty. We reached Los Gatos at one o'clock; stopped at the boarding-house. I took a room, and after washing and brushing for a half hour, began to look once more like a civilized person. After taking a late lunch I took up my basket once more, and started for the store; here I met two young gentlemen, who promised to buy Mark Twain's "Gilded Age" when I was here before. In speaking to them concerning the book, they said they had not forgotten our agreement, which was: I was to let them have the leather binding for the same price as the cloth. Having none but the cloth binding, we had some joking and disagreement about the price; but we settled it, and they took the books.

Mr. H. came in during the conversation, and told how he once made a raise by selling books. "I was down to the bed-rock," as the Californians say. "As I could not get any other employment, concluded to try canvassing for the Life of Lincoln, in Santa Clara County. In going from Saratoga to Los Gatos, across the country, I lost my way. Stopping at Mr. P's. to make inquiry, I tried to sell him a book; he would not buy, and I could not make him believe I had lost my way. He said, 'You are pretty smart, but you can't play lost on me.' He insisted upon my staying all night, saying he would like to have an argument with me about the war. Thanking him, I bade him good evening without gaining the desired information. I soon found the road, and reached Los Gatos soon after dark, where I stopped for the night." Mr. H. also said "there was a great deal of money made by *some* canvassers; still, for all that, it is the most trying business I ever engaged in. But ladies do better than gentlemen, I think, as they are not likely to be treated so abruptly." I replied " that they were not so used to battling with the world, and their trials were far greater. We will not argue the question now; I must be going." I could not get him to subscribe for a book, although he said he would like to, but did not feel able.

Leaving my basket and books in his store, I started out on foot for the ranche. On my way I called on Mrs. M. She has lived in this neighborhood for many years. She does not like ranching, and thinks I would not either; but I think differently. I would prefer any place that was quiet to this excitable life I am now leading. After a few moments more conversation I bade her good afternoon.

In going along the road I passed Mrs. F's. almond orchard. I could not but notice how nicely it was kept, and how fine the trees were looking. Crossed the road, passed through the gate, and was now at the place I expected to make my future home. At present it looks very dismal and forsaken. Still through time it can be made very comfortable. Mrs. C. and myself walked around the place, she telling me not to be afraid to move on it, as we could make a good living. After making some calculation concerning repairs, returned to the store. Taking my basket and books, I called on Mr. R., at his residence; was introduced to his wife and son; found them very pleasant. The latter bought Mark Twain's "Gilded Age." Thanking him, and it now being dark, hastened to the boarding house. There I found one of my fellow passengers of the morning stage seated in the sitting room, and soon learned he was from Terre Haute, Indiana; was traveling for pleasure. Having heard so much about California and its beautiful climate, he thought he would like to spend a season here. It was two weeks since he arrived; so far as he had seen, he was very much pleased with the country; but said he would not like to make it his home, on account of the society. I told him he must not judge too hastily, when he inquired how long I had lived here; upon telling him six years, he said, "Well, madam, do you think the society here is as good as it is in the Eastern States?" I replied, "It is not to be expected, as California is settled with different nationalities, from all parts of the globe, and they are constantly changing from one place to another. I can see a great change in society since I came here, for the better.

"When the population becomes permanently located the society will be as refined as it is now in the East. There is one thing I can say, there is no State in the Union where you will find as many kind and benevolent people as in California. At least I have always found them so. I think you will form the same opinion, after you have been here one season." To which he replied, "Probably I shall." The conversation turned on different subjects, until time for retiring.

Upon waking, next morning, I did not feel very much refreshed; having coughed all the fore part of the night. I think it must have been from inhaling dust the day previous. After eating breakfast, I took my basket of books, and canvassed the large City of Los Gatos, consisting of five dwelling houses, two stores, and a blacksmiths' shop. Oh, I had forgotten also a Chinese wash house. I could not help but stop and admire their vegetable garden. 'Tis astonishing what a quantity of vegetables they will raise on such a small piece of ground. They are certainly a very energetic and industrious race of people. Still I think they are a greater curse to our country than ever slavery was. I may be wrong.

Returning to the boarding house at noon, I packed my traps, took a hasty lunch, settled my bill, and went to the company's store to wait for the Santa Cruz stage, which leaves at one o'clock. Picking up my satchel, I found a card tied to it, with the words written on it, "Mrs. A. J. L., &c. Book Peddler. Beware of her." I took it good naturedly, and laughed heartily with the rest of them. The stage at last drives up, being a few minutes late. Taking a seat inside, everything ready, we start. Passing the Ten Mile House, we commenced ascending the mountains; the stage stopped at Lexington to change horses, and for the passengers to take lunch. In half an hour we are off again.

The scenery now becomes very grand. Although I had traveled over the road once before, still I saw new beauties in every place. The first time the mountains and deep ravines were covered with wild flowers. Then it was spring; now it is mid-summer. There are but few flowers to be seen, but the tall and stately redwood, pine and madrona mingled with many other varieties, with here and there a high rough stone or cragged peak; now and then you caught a glimpse of a small valley, dotted with farm houses; all combining to make the scenery grand and picturesque. As we neared the top of the mountains we met the person known as Mountain Charley; the stage stops while he tells the driver the sad news of his son's death, and how it occurred—having shot himself accidentally. I watched him closely during the conversation. Though used to the hardships of a mountaineer's life, I could see with what an iron will he kept back the tears. A parent's love was there. He passed on, looking very sad. The stage now moves very slowly. The soil presents a white, ashy appearance, with here and there a tree, and very few shrubs. This only continues a very short time; we now begin to descend the mountains. The scenery is, if anything, grander than on the other side. But the horses are driven with such rapidity, making such quick and short turns, it is impossible to look around very much, without becoming dizzy; though I enjoyed the view very much. We passed through a small valley, which, upon inquiry, I found to be Scott's Valley. Horses are changed again, and we lose some of our passengers, four in number, making the rest of the drive rougher than ever. Santa Cruz is reached about five o'clock. I stopped at the Santa Cruz house, very tired and dusty, thinking wasn't it jolly to be a book agent. About this time I caught a glimpse of myself in the mirror in my room, and laughed right heartily at my appearance. My face and hair were completely covered with dust, with the exception of a streak here and there on my cheek, that I had brushed away in moving my veil, reminding me of ladies I had seen who had powdered their faces so thickly that when they perspired it left their faces streaked, or some urchin with a very dirty face had cried, and the tears had run down his cheeks, leaving a clean place; but enough of this nonsense. With the free use of water and soap I began to look like myself again, and felt much refreshed. I then descended to the dining-room.

I went to the sitting-room, where I passed a pleasant evening with the landlady, finding out many points concerning my business for the morrow.

At nine o'clock next morning, I started for the Court House; found but one office opened. A gentleman was seated at his desk, reading a paper. I had never met him before, and supposed from his actions that he was a deputy. I inquired of him for Mr. B——. He told me that he had not been re-elected last fall. I then took out the "Life of Sumner" from my basket, and asked him if he would not like to buy a copy, to which he replied, "No, madam, I have vowed I never would buy another book from an agent. In the first place, they charge twice as much as they are worth; and another thing, they are generally nothing but a lot of trash." I answered: "I think you are mistaken, sir; there are many good and valuable books sold by subscription."

"There is no use arguing. When I wish a book I will go to the store and buy it. Just the other day there was a nice young lady came in and persuaded me to subscribe. In a few days she brought the book; it is the most trashy thing I ever read." I learned afterward he did not buy the book at all; that his clerk bought it and gave it to him.

Many others passed in and out; among them Mr. C—. I was very glad to meet him, as I had not forgotten his kindness to me when I was here last fall. After conversing for a little while, he asked me what books I had this time. I told him several; among them, the "Life of Sumner," and "Johnson's Sketches of the War." After looking them over, said he could not buy this time, as he had been getting married. "My wife needs all my spare coin. But if I can assist you in any other way I shall be pleased to do so."

By this time the offices were all opened. I went down the hall to Mr. M—'s room. He received me very kindly; looked at all my books; said he would like to have Johnson's work. "Call and see my wife, as she buys all the books, and knows better what kind she would like." I told him I never canvassed among the ladies in this place. I had tried it in many other towns without good success. "You will not find it so here," he replied. "They are the principal ones that buy; at least, my wife always does. You call on her and see. I would like to have her patronize you, because I believe you deserve it, unless you have deceived me. If you have, that remains with you and your God." I reassured him my statements were correct.

Promising to call on his wife in the afternoon, I crossed the hall to Mr. J. G's room. He was kind, but begged to be excused, as he was very busy; telling me to call again. Saying I would do so, I thanked him, and left the Court House, thinking how different his words were from the gentleman's I had first met. Mr. J. G's were kind, with a touch of pity in them, while the other one's were harsh, and inclined to be sarcastic, as though "You are nothing but a book agent." I feel these things very keenly, though I know mine is an honorable and legitimate business, and no *lady* or *gentleman* would look at it in any other light; and God knows I try to conduct myself in such a way as to command respect from all. I called on many others, with little or no success. Mr. L. said he would not subscribe, but he would buy Sumner's book when I delivered it. My next visit was to the telegraph office, where I sent an order to Romans' for some books. It was now noon. After lunch I called on Mrs. L., at her residence across the creek. As I passed up the walk, I could not help but admire the beautiful grounds. The bell was answered by a neat looking lady, whom I found to be Mrs. L. When I told her my business, she said her husband was speaking about me at lunch time. I accepted her kind offer to walk in and rest myself, while she examined the books. She bought Johnson's work, and subscribed for "Poetry and Songs," by William Cullen Bryant. Thanking her for her kindness and patronage, I crossed the road to a building I found to be a beer saloon. The proprietor tried to get me into an argument on local option. I told him I would not express my opinion either way.

"You women, tramping around the country, are generally in favor of woman's rights." I replied, "local option and woman's rights have nothing to do with each other. I am in favor of the latter, with regard to labor. I think a lady can be a lady, and follow any occupation. If she does her duty and performs the same labor as a gentleman, she ought to receive the same pay for it. But I do not believe in the ladies having the ballot. If they had it, their votes would not be so easily bought as some men's are." I left him, and crossed the street again; called at a great many different dwellings, and was treated politely by all; but made no sales. Found several who had already purchased Sumner's book. Leaving the hill, I crossed the creek, and started for the hotel. As I passed up the street, two gentlemen were seated in front of a store. To my asking them to buy, they replied, as many others have done, "I cannot read." "You are to be pitied," I said, and passed on to the hotel.

My first thoughts are, this morning, must I move in the current, wear a smile, while my heart is sad? Making a hasty toilet, I descended to the breakfast table, where the landlady introduced me to Mr. A. We talked on different subjects. I asked him if he could tell me Mr. B's. office hours. Instead of informing me, he said, abruptly, "Why, I attend to all the business. He does the *head* work, and I handle the money. I am the money part of the institution." I replied, "It is the money I am after," thinking he needed some one to do the head work for him. "I have several books. I should like to sell you and Mr. B. a copy. Mr. A's. countenance fell. "You can't sell me any books; I don't know what you can do with Mr. B." He then turned from me, and commenced telling the landlady how he intended to enlarge his house; and that was the way he thought of spending his money. I went to my room, thinking it sad to be a book agent, especially when you meet gentlemen who have the handling of other people's money.

I started for Mr. C's. drug store; found him very jovial, and glad to see me; saying he had bought a book the other day, and would like to trade with me. I said I was in for a trade, if it was not too much soiled, and he would give me boot enough. We were interrupted by the entrance of Mr. C., an insurance agent. We had met often before in our travels. After shaking hands, he said, "Mrs. L., don't you think book and insurance agents have a hard time? I am afraid I shall never get to Heaven, for the fibs I have told." Then he went on to illustrate some of them. In trying to get them to insure their lives, he would tell them how Mr. Smith, Brown or Jones got blown up in some mill, or crushed in the cars, and would have left his family destitute, if it was not for the insurance he had on his life. Some of them are foolish enough to believe it true; when it is all hearsay. I do not know how much longer he would have kept on this strain, but on looking out, I saw the 'bus was ready to start for the beach, and not wishing to miss it, I left the store, and took a seat inside, with many more. On our way the driver stopped; an elderly lady with two boys, both using crutches, got in. They looked like brothers. I thought how sad it was to see them so afflicted, not being able to run about like other children; although they looked happy. By the time the 'bus reached the beach, it was pretty well filled. I went with the crowd into the sitting-room of the lower bath house. The sitting-room was well filled with different nationalities, from the Caucasian race to the African. It was now ten o'clock, the time for surf bathing. I wandered up and down the beach, in hopes of getting a glimpse of the masked bather. My curiosity was not gratified. Afterwards I visited the upper bath-house.

I do not find any pleasure in wandering alone, for

those I love are not with me to enjoy the scene. I took lunch at the last mentioned bath house. Ascending the hill, I called at Mr. W's warehouse; tried to sell Mr. G. a book, but with no success. Mr. W. and wife drove up to the door in a buggy. I tried them, and both refused. After calling at every house in that vicinity, and not getting any orders, I concluded to return to the hotel. After waiting for some time, and not seeing any prospect of getting a conveyance, I started on foot. I stopped at several residences on my way, but I might as well not have gone in, as it availed me nothing. At the hotel I left my basket, and went around to the express office, to see if my books had come; they had not. Being greatly disappointed, and knowing there must have been some mistake in the dispatch, or they would have filled my order, I tried to find the telegraph operator; but could not. It being late, I concluded to wait until morning.

At eight o'clock next morning I found him, and learned there was a mistake, through the Watsonville office.

As it would detain me too long to have another order sent to this place, I sent an order for the books to be sent to Watsonville. I then called on all who had subscribed, and got them to wait for their books until October. It was now twelve o'clock. As the stage did not leave for S. for several hours yet, I busied myself in writing up Santa Cruz.

Four o'clock found me in S. The landlady at the hotel was very sick. I was shown to my room by a woman in charge, whom I had met when I was there before. She said, "Our town is overrun with book agents; we are all getting pretty tired of them. There was one old woman here, selling her life, or some other kind of a book, written by herself. When she came, she said she was going to stop here; but did not. I don't know what became of her, nor I don't care." I smiled, and thought to myself, "When I am gone, won't I catch it." She turned very abruptly, saying, "I hope you will be comfortable in this room. I must go;" and *she went*. Wasn't I *sorry?* Arranging my traps, I took up my basket and started for the tannery. Trudging along through the dust, from two to six inches deep, I passed Mr. S—'s saloon, and got his order for Joseph E. Johnson's work. At the tannery there were but three or four men at work; one of them told me the firm had "busted" up. They could not buy, because they would be out of work in a few days. I called at several private residences; found the ladies agreeable, neat and tidy housekeepers. I returned by the way of the blacksmith shop; the gentleman promised to buy a book when I came back in the fall. Called at the store, but had no success; crossed the street to the telegraph office; sold one of Mark Twain's "Gilded Age" to the operator, who, by the way, I found to be a very kind hearted gentleman. I next called on the butcher. He recognized me immediately, and seemed very glad to see me, but would not buy.

I stayed all night at the hotel. In the morning the stage from Santa Cruz arrived, bound for Watsonville. On the middle seat were two young ladies and one gentleman. I said I could not ride backwards, at which the gentleman arose and gave me *his* seat; for it, I thanked him.

The stage moved on; the two young ladies kept the passengers laughing for some time, by the description they gave a gentleman as to how they intended to marry some old man for his money. "Of course," said one, "he would not want to go to parties, balls, and such places, being well enough satisfied with our smiles during the day. He could stay at home, and take care of the house and children, if there were any, while we would take his purse and some *young* man's arm, and go to a ball or place of amusement. We would *have* to take his purse, because the young gentlemen nowadays have no money, and some of them very little brains. I don't know but two or three, in all my acquaintances, that can make a living for themselves, much less a wife. But they are, most of them, jolly good fellows to go around with."

The other one now spoke up, saying, "I had my heart set on Mr. M. R.; but understood, the other day, he was so stingy he would not eat a square meal. That almost frightened me, for I tell you I like good grub; still, he has so much money, is so tall, so *handsome*, and so *very* polite, I scarcely know how to express my feelings."

"Will you allow me to express mine, Miss, with regard to his politeness?" I said. To which she replied, "Certainly." "I called at his office, some time ago, in San Francisco. He reminded me of some savage, snarly bull dog, keeping watch over some bones that he could not eat himself, nor would not allow any other dog to, without a big fight. When I addressed him, all the answer I got was a snarl. He *might* have been very polite and sociable, had he not seen I was a book-agent. Perhaps he thought they ought not to expect politeness from anyone." In reply to this, she said, "just wait until I get him; I will train him to do differently; at least, I think so. I have never had the pleasure of seeing him yet."

13

After a few more jests, we arrive in front of the hotel in Watsonville. Here I part with my companions; they going on to San Jose, and I remaining at the hotel.

CHAPTER XVIII.

Watsonville.

This is my second visit here; not having much success the first time, I started out with but little energy. At the express office I found my box of books awaiting me. I took two, and started out again on my regular canvass. Soon sold them, and received several more orders. In the afternoon, while in conversation with a gentleman from the country, some one passed, whom he called Judge. He said, "This lady has some books for sale; would you like to purchase a copy?" He replied, "I cannot read." I told him I did not like to hear any one make light of education, for I had worked the life almost out of me to educate my children, and did not like to hear it made fun of. He looked at me very solemnly, and said, "I am sorry you wern't around when I was a child." By this time there were several present; they all laughed heartily. I took it good-naturedly, and laughed with the rest; but succeeded in persuading some of them to subscribe for a book. Leaving them, I went up stairs into a lawyer's room; was treated very kindly, but could not get him to buy.

Passing into the street, I saw three or four gentlemen in a group. Approaching them, I asked, "Gentlemen, will you allow me to show you some books that are for sale?" They all answered politely they did not wish to buy; but one ruffian straightened himself very proudly, and said, "I have too many children to buy school books for; they are scattered all around; I expect to be elected mayor of this town; so I can father all the hoodlums running abroad." He laughed, thinking he had said something very smart. I told him I guessed his mother had died before he could remember her. From his looks and actions, one would think he was capable of being father to a hoodlum. I now returned to the hotel, where I spent a very pleasant evening in the parlor, listening to some fine music by a professor from San Francisco, who was staying in the country for his health. Next day, being Sunday, I spent the greater part of it in my room, writing.

Monday morning I started to work with new energies, being somewhat refreshed with my day's rest. I called on Mr. B., where I met a gentleman who tried to joke me about Masonry and Odd Fellowship. Found I was well posted, and acknowledged I had a right to wear the emblems. Returned to the hotel and took the hack for the railroad depot.

BOUND FOR SALINAS CITY.

The country through which the cars passed did not impress me very favorably, portions of it being low and swampy; although in some places there seemed to be excellent soil, and finer crops I never saw. In conversation with a gentleman on the train, I was told, upon inquiry, that the Abbott House was the best hotel in the place.

Arriving there, I took the coach, and was driven to the hotel before mentioned. I found it to be as fine and well kept as any I had seen in so small a place. I was shown to a room in the third story, neatly furnished, and very pleasant.

Arranging my baggage, I took my basket, and once more became book agent. As I passed through the hall I noticed it was just five minutes to three. At the foot of the stairs I paused to think which way I had better go. Though I had canvassed for almost six years, I was now in a strange place, and must meet strange faces. My thoughts were, "how will they treat me; will they meet me kindly or abruptly?" With a heavy heart I stepped into the street. I made inquiries for the Court House; being told, I started in that direction. On my way I passed the post office; stepped in, and found a letter from home waiting for me.

I once more started for the Court House. Found the building not very prepossessing in its appearance. I first called on Mr. D. He was very polite and kind; but after talking some time, I could not induce him to buy a book. In the same office was Mr. S.; he spoke very crossly: " Am very busy, and don't wish you to bother me," is his reply in answer to my asking him if he would like to subscribe for Charles Sumner's Life. I next called on Mr. A.; found him pleasant, and promised to buy a book when I came in October. Thanking him, I passed into the next room, where I found four gentlemen very busily writing, and one other, (making five in all) who had a more elevated seat than the rest, and seemed to be giving orders. Although not very tall, he was somewhat like the Dutch girl, pretty wide out. Book agent addressed him; good looking man looked up, smiled, and asked: "What do you wish, madam?" " I have some books I would like to show you." At this his countenance fell wonderfully, and he replied: "I am too poor to buy." I insisted upon his buying, when he turned very abruptly, and inquired my name. I told him I was not ashamed of it; it was Mrs. L.; whereupon he looked at the other gentleman, and introduced me to the *Judge*, so *he* said; which seemed to occasion great laughter, much to my annoyance. Good looking man could not but see I was annoyed, for he is a "*Judy*." I suppose he thought, as I was only a book agent, he could have all the fun he desired, at my expense; so he went on, making his eloquent speeches, while I stepped back, and stood in perfect amazement. I have sat for hours listening to the ablest lawyers, pleading for criminals, but never did I hear anything half so *grand* or *eloquent* as his little speech was. While he was talking he kept backing toward the door, until he passed out. I sighed to think I did not learn his name; perhaps we may meet again. After showing the book to the remaining four gentlemen, and getting one order for "Sumner's Life," I thanked them and left the room, returning to the hotel, where I spent the remainder of the evening.

Next morning I wrote for a few hours, and started once more for the Court House, for I wished to see the rest of the County officers. Made my way to the Judge's room, where I found five or six gentlemen writing. One of them I had frequently met in San Francisco during my canvassing. He seemed to recognize me, and said, abruptly, "What brought you here?" I will call him City Gent. While I was engaged in showing my books to the rest of the gentlemen, City Gent spoke, and asked me if I knew Tom Collins. "No," said I, "what about him?" City Gent, "Why, yes, you know **Tom Collins**, of San Francisco." I replied I knew several gentlemen by the name of Collins, but did not know Tom. I looked around the room at each gentleman's countenance, to learn his meaning; but their faces betrayed nothing. City Gent, "Upon my word and honor, he is here in town hunting you." In reply to my question, "What does he wish?" he said, "He has a dispatch for you from home." I told him I did not believe a word of it. My family knew where I was, and would telegraph to me. There was a smart young gent, very dark complexioned, and not very tall, in the office, who, with a hateful grin, said. "Yes, madam, you go ask the telegraph operator if Tom Collins didn't get a dispatch for you." I replied, "Thank you, sir; don't trouble yourself; I will attend to my own business. I do not wish to jest about it, because I might get one that would cause me great trouble."

On my way to Mr. C. A's. room, I must acknowledge I was somewhat worried; still I believed they were trying to play some kind of a joke on me. I found Mr. C. A. in; he told me to be seated while he examined the books. I asked him if he knew of such a person as Tom Collins. He smiled, and said, "They have been trying to play Tom Collins on you, have they?" He then told me the joke. I was hurt and annoyed, to think I had to contend with all classes; and could not restrain my tears. But I soon dried them, thinking what a fool I was to allow myself to take any notice of it. Mr. C. A. signed for a book, and tried to cheer me, with many kind words. We conversed about the Southern people, and their trials; of the war and its many sorrows. I bade him good day, and left the room in better spirits than I had entered.

On my way to the hotel I called at Mr. W's. office, who is a fat, jolly man. There were several gentlemen in; one of them bought Joseph E. Johnson's book. Expressing my thanks, I started again for the hotel. As I passed through the dining-room, all eyes seemed upon me. I imagined they thought "there goes the book agent they tried to play Tom Collins on," because nearly all of the gentlemen were at the different tables eating, that were in the office at the time. After being seated at the table, there was some little jesting about the Tom Collins affair, between Mr. B., his wife and myself. Returning to my room, I found Mrs. B. in the hall; she wanted to know the particulars about the joke. I related the facts concerning it, also the circumstances under which I had met the city gent heretofore, and his impoliteness towards me. She said from what she had heard about him, he was no gentleman. I passed into the street, and stopped at the large grocery on the corner. After urging the proprietor for some time to buy, and not succeeding, I went into the office, to see the book keeper. When I addressed him, he looked very blank as though he did not know anything. I told him I had the "Life of Sumner," and "Johnson's Narrative of the War." He took both order-books in his hands, as though he was so weak he could scarcely hold them. "Who is Sumner, and who is Johnson?" he drawled out; "I never heard of them." Looking up at me, he said again, "Are they some great men in San Francisco?" I replied, "Sir, I pity you very much, for being so ignorant." He saw I knew he was trying to play smart, and said, "Excuse me, madam; but I cannot buy either." I next visited many private families, but without success.

In front of the hotel I met Mr. C— of San Jose. After shaking hands with him, the proprietor came up. He was well acquainted with Mr. C., and slightly with me. Laughing, he said, "Well, Mrs. L., they did'nt play Tom Collins on you." "No," I said, "I am too much of a Yankee; am too inquisitive to be caught by such sharpers." The proprietor was then called away, and Mr. C— asked me what was the trouble. I related to him the circumstance of the morning. The city gent was sitting near, and heard our conversation. He came forward and said, "Madam, I do not wish you to be angry with me; indeed, upon my word and honor, I did not mean to play a joke on you."

"Please stop, sir, and do not tell another falsehood." He said, "Why did you tell that lady about me? I'll have no chance with them." "Sir, what need you care for the ladies? you have a wife already; at least I judge so, from what I have heard."

"It makes no difference whether I have or have not; I always treated you well; have I not?"

"There are two questions I should like to ask you; can you give me a truthful answer?"

Upon his saying he could, I said, "You have met me a great many times at different places, and under different circumstances. Did you ever know or hear of any harm of me?" "No," he answered, "I have always heard you highly spoken of, as being a hard working, industrious woman."

"Did you ever know me to tell a falsehood?" "No." "Then, I did not tell that lady one either." He looked at Mr. C—, winked, and said, "I do not know when I ever misused you, unless it was when you had some books or pictures; will you please name any one time when I treated you badly?"

"You have urged it on me; I can tell you very plainly, that I have never met you at any place that I found you a gentleman; always rough and uncouth. The first time was in a lawyer's office in the city, when I was canvassing for the upright picture of the Grant Family. When I showed it to you, you very abruptly told me you would buy it, if it had all his family on it, including his squaw wife and Indian babies. The second time, from your personal appearance, and the appearance of your office, I saw you were going down: although you *treated* me ungentlemanly, I *pitied* you very much; since that time, I have seen you in the street cars, and doubted if you knew where you were."

At all this he replied, "Let's shake hands, and be friends." "I have no objections, but I should think an old grey haired man like you would be ashamed to trifle with an old grey haired woman like I am." By this time there was quite a crowd gathered around us. Thinking I was making myself too conspicuous in a strange place, I went to my room, tired and disgusted. In the morning I called on Mr. F.—. He gave me an order for William H. Seward's "Travels around the World."

On my way back to the hotel I again met Mr. C— of San José. I asked him if he thought I did wrong in talking to the city gent as I did. "No, I think you did just right," he said; "but knowing you as well as I do, I must acknowledge I was somewhat astonished at your courage; but still you kept even with him."

I next went to the Express office, and had my box of books sent to San Jose. I returned to my room to wait until time to go to the depot. Bidding adieu to one and all, I left Salinas City; but sigh to think I did not learn the good looking man's name. As I have described this part of the country in another chapter, I shall not repeat it, although seeing new beauties in every place. At Gilroy we stopped to take lunch. A little ways from the station the conductor came around to collect the fare; in the far end of the car was a very dark Spanish boy, from ten to fourteen years old. When the conductor asked him for his ticket, he said his mother had it. "Where is your mother?" He raised up, and pointed to where I was sitting. "Come along, and show me." He coolly walked down the aisle, stopped in front of my seat, and without flinching, said, "Mother, I want my ticket, or six bits."

The conductor being well acquainted with me, knew he was lying, and pushed him down into a seat opposite, saying, "Boy, I know that lady; she is not your mother;" but he still persisted I was, and it was some time before he would acknowledge that his mother was not on the train. The gentleman sitting behind me said, "wasn't that the coolest piece of impudence you ever saw?" It was such a good joke on me that it was soon whispered among the passengers, and caused great laughter and merriment all the way to San Jose.

On my arrival there, I went directly to Mrs. B., where I remained twenty-four hours. After delivering my books, and collecting what was due me, I went to Santa Clara, and remained all night. Next morning I took the early train for Redwood City. When I went to the hotel I met my old friend, the bachelor, looking much better than I expected to see; for I had *heard* he was very sick. After a short and pleasant conversation, I started out to deliver my books. Calling at Mr. C—'s blacksmith shop, he insisted upon my going around to see his wife, as they had moved in his new house. I told him I should be very much pleased to do so; but did not think I should have time. Here I received several orders for my *own* book. At the mill I delivered some books, and got some new orders. It was, by this time, twelve o'clock. I remained at the hotel until time to take the cars for home. Bidding my friends good bye, I left Redwood City, and was once more on my way to San Francisco. When the train left the former place, it was a bright, sunny afternoon; as it neared the city the wind blew cold; and at San Miguel the fog was very heavy. At the junction of Fourth & Folsom St. R. R. I met my husband on his way home from the office. When I got home I found a nice hot dinner awaiting me. Seated at the table, I am thankful that I am home again, and find them all well.

EXPLANATIONS.

I hope all who may have read this simple sketch will not criticise it too severely, but remember it was hastily written; the authoress a plain, unassuming, hard working woman; not aspiring for fame or popularity, but wishing to show how rough and impolite many persons act towards the class of people so called " Book Agents," forgetting it is an honorable occupation, if properly conducted; and politeness costs nothing. No agent, that is a true lady or gentleman, will urge their books upon any one; some people think no respectable person would go around the street peddling books ; but they are very much mistaken.

I know *some* who have canvassed that were *once* surrounded by all the luxuries money could buy, but when these were swept away, sunshiny friends had flown; they felt the cold hand of poverty grasping them, and would sell books sooner than be supported by charity; through all never forgetting for a moment that they were ladies.

I ask pardon of my readers if they *think* I have been too sarcastic in some of my remarks; many may think me malicious, but I have no malice toward anyone, nor have I written untruly with regard to anything; and many times beside those mentioned have had my feelings hurt so severely, I wept bitterly. Still there is no business but what has its trials; and this one, I suppose, is no exception. In the six years I have canvassed I can truthfully say, taking the ladies and gentlemen as a majority, they have treated me with great respect and patronized me liberally, for which I offer, to one and all, my sincere thanks, and hope they may prosper in all their undertakings.

Respectfully yours,
J. W. L.

www.ingramcontent.com/pod-product-compliance
Lightning Source LLC
Chambersburg PA
CBHW032152160426
43197CB00008B/872